RELIGIOUS MINORITIES IN CANADA
A Sociological Study of the Japanese Experience

Mark Mullins

Canadian Studies
Volume 4

The Edwin Mellen Press
Lewiston/Queenston/Lampeter

Library of Congress Cataloging-in-Publication Data

Mullins, Mark.
    Religious minorities in Canada : a sociological study of the
Japanese experience / by Mark Mullins.
        p. cm. -- (Canadian studies ; v. 4)
    Bibliography: p.
    Includes index.
    ISBN 0-88946-195-3
    1. Japanese--Canada--Religion. 2. Canada--Religion. I. Title.
    II. Series: Canadian studies (Lewiston, N.Y.) ; v. 4.
BL2530.C2M85 1988
306' .6' 089956071--dc19   88-1703
                                                                      CIP

| This is volume 4 in the continuing series |
| Canadian Studies |
| Volume 4 ISBN 0-88946-195-3 |
| CS Series ISBN 0-88946-197-X |

The Edwin Mellen Press   The Edwin Mellen Press
Box 450   Box 67
Lewiston, NY   Queenston, Ontario
USA   14092   CANADA   L0S 1L0

The Edwin Mellen Press
Mellen House
Lampeter, Dyfed
Wales, U.K.
SA48 7DY

Printed in the United States of America

CONTENTS

LIST OF ILLUSTRATIONS

List of Figures

List of Tables

PREFACE

Just over a decade ago, Hiller (1976) could safely write that the sociological study of Canadian religion "is still in embryonic form." Although valuable studies have appeared since this assessment was made, many aspects of Canadian religious life have yet to receive systematic study by sociologists.

This present volume is intended as a modest contribution to this developing discipline in a twofold sense. First, this study elaborates and applies a typology of minority churches initially designed to aid in the analysis of Canadian religion. Millett (1969) showed that the typology was a useful tool for identifying and classifying forms of religion in Canada which had been neglected in the previously used categories of church, sect, and cult (Clark, 1948; Mann, 1956). In the following pages the additional potential of this typology for the study of ethnic organizational dynamics will be explored.

Second, this volume provides a case study of religion in the Japanese Canadian community. Readers should recognize that the aim of this work is not to provide an ethnographic description of Japanese religious consciousness in Canada. Rather, it is to describe and analyze the organizational development of Japanese churches. Hopefully, this study of one of Canada's "visible minorities" will increase our understanding of the nature of religious pluralism in contemporary society. Moreover, it will clarify the multicultural nature of Canadian society. What happens to the religion of ethnic minorities after several generations in Canada? Is the "ethnic mosaic" a reality and does the policy of multiculturalism encourage ethnic persistence? The findings of this study on Japanese Canadians should reveal something about the nature of this host society and be suggestive of the future of other ethnic minorities in Canada.

The material for this monograph was collected over a four-year period (1981-1984). I would like to express appreciation to McMaster University for generous travel grants that made it possible for me to pursue field research across Canada.

This study would not have been possible without the kind cooperation of many Japanese Canadians--too many, in fact, to name here. Priests, ministers, and active lay leaders of Japanese churches throughout Canada were generous with their time and made available to me important materials needed for this study. I will long remember their warm hospitality and hours of conversation.

I gratefully acknowledge the assistance of several archivists in locating materials relevant to my research: Mr. George Brandak, Special Collections Division, University of British Columbia; Mr. Bob Stewart, United Church Archives, Vancouver School of Theology; and Mr. N. Semple, United Church Archives, Victoria University, Toronto.

About ten years ago I was introduced to the sociology of religion in a seminar on New Religious Movements at Regent College taught by Irving Hexham (now on the faculty of the University of Calgary). At the time, of course, I had no idea that this field of study would become my major preoccupation. I wish to express my gratitude for his longstanding friendship and for his encouragement as I have continued research in this area.

I am also indebted to a number of persons for their encouragement and critical response to my research and writing on Japanese Canadians over the past few years. Among these individuals are Robert Blumstock, Louis Greenspan, William Shaffir, W.J. Slater (all of McMaster University), and Mitsuru Shimpo (St. Jerome's College, University of Waterloo).

Finally, I would like to acknowledge the assistance I received from my wife, Cindy. Her careful reading of several drafts and editorial suggestions have improved this manuscript considerably. As a small token of my gratitude, this work is affectionately dedicated to her.

Shikoku Christian College
Zentsuji, Japan
May 1987

CHAPTER ONE: THE STUDY OF MINORITY CHURCHES

Introduction

The study of religious organizations has long been an important focus of investigation within the sociology of religion. The dominant perspective guiding research in this area developed out of the church-sect typology originally formulated by Weber and Troeltsch. Since the typology was first utilized in the study of religion in North America (see, Niebuhr, 1929; Clark, 1948), there have been numerous attempts to refine the basic categories of analysis. Over the past several decades most of these efforts have been preoccupied with the nature of Protestant sectarianism and have neglected other types of religious organizations equally important in Canada and the United States.

Some years ago Bryan Wilson, the foremost sociologist of sectarianism, wrote that: "If the sociology of religion is to move forward, we must create categories which allow us to study comparatively the social functions and development of religious movements" (1969:361). Sub-typologies of sects have been elaborated and our understanding of the dynamics of sect development has advanced.[1] Similar refinements of the church-type, however, "have been few and unprofitable" (Beckford, 1974:98).

Recognizing the inadequacy of existing schemes of classification for the study of religion in Canada, Millett (1969; 1971) proposed a typology of minority churches. The concept "minority church" was initially designed by Roger Mehl, a French theologian and sociologist, to aid in the analysis of religious

minorities in various European countries. Observing the
marginal position of Protestants in France, Spain, and
Italy, Mehl recognized that minority churches without
the same legal status and political rights of the
dominant religious institutions are under continual
pressure to become sects. This pressure is usually
resisted, he explains, because minority churches have a
larger reference group which relativizes their marginal
status in society.[2]

Millett found that the minority church sub-type
could be fruitfully applied to the study of religion in
Canada. In his analysis of Canadian Census data he
observed that approximately 90 percent of the population
conformed to "church-like" behavior. Thus, a more
adequate analysis of religion in Canada would require
that some distinctions be made "within the huge category
known as 'churches'" (1969:112). Millett then used the
minority church sub-type to identify hundreds of ethnic
congregations in Canada.

The minority status of these churches is related to
two issues. First, they operate in a non-official
language. Second, they are not self-sufficient; that
is, they are dependent upon a parent organization for
leadership and authority in religious matters. Millett
divided these minority churches into two classes:
"foreign-oriented" and "native-oriented" (1969:113).
Foreign-oriented minority churches are defined as those
ethnic organizations which are linked to a mother church
in the old country; consequently, their primary
reference group is outside Canada. Native-oriented
minority churches are those ethnic organizations
operating in non-official languages which are sponsored
by an indigenous Canadian church.[3]

In his review of sociological studies of religious organizations, Beckford recognized the value of Millett's sub-typology for clarifying the Canadian Census data on religion. He went on to point out, however, that "its relevance for the strictly organizational aspects of religious groups has yet to be demonstrated" (1974:99). One aim of this case study of Japanese religion in Canada is to explore the additional potential of this sub-typology as a tool for organizational analysis. Before further elaboration of this typological framework, it is important to place this study within the broader theoretical context of perspectives on religion and ethnicity.

Religion and Ethnicity: Theoretical Background

It is widely recognized that religion and ethnicity are closely related phenomena in North America. In fact, the story of religion in the New World has been largely shaped by patterns of immigration and the establishment of various ethnic traditions (Herberg, 1955:10; Handy, 1975:5). Most sociological assessments of the relationship between religion and ethnicity usually follow two general interpretations.

One major perspective on this relationship emphasizes the conservative role of religion in maintaining ethnic customs, language, and group solidarity. This approach is clearly reminiscent of Durkheim's (1965) functionalist theory of religion. Religious beliefs and rituals, he maintained, bind individuals together and provide the social context necessary for the transmission of traditions and values. A number of sociologists have recently emphasized the traditional functions and integrative consequences of

religion for ethnic groups in modern pluralistic
societies. Millett, for example, writes:

> One observation occurs repeatedly as one
> studies various ethnic groups in Canada: of
> all the institutions supporting the survival
> of distinctive cultures, the church is
> usually the strongest and the most active
> (1975:105).

Similarly, Mol notes that:

> In the countries of immigration, migrant
> churches have always been the most effective
> bastions of ethnic preservation (1976:174).

The conservative functions of religion in relation to
ethnicity have been summarized at greater length by
Anderson and Frideres:

> Many of the functions of religion are
> oriented toward the preservation of ethnic
> identity. As various social scientists have
> pointed out, religion contributes to a sense
> of identity in an age of depersonalization;
> it may be a nationalistic force and assume
> the role of the protector of ethnic identity;
> it promotes social integration; it attempts
> to validate a people's customs and values
> through socialization; it affirms the
> dignity of ethnic group members who might be
> considered by non-members as having low
> status; it tends to be a pillar of
> conservatism; and it often encourages
> conscious social isolation from outsiders
> (1981:41).

Few sociologists would deny that religion is often oriented toward the maintenance of ethnicity. What has not been adequately analyzed, however, is the long-term effectiveness of ethnic churches as agents of cultural preservation. In order to determine their actual role and effectiveness a cross-generational study is necessary. A review of the literature on religion and ethnicity reveals a lack of studies analyzing religio-ethnic behavior through successive generations.[4]

A second perspective on religion and ethnicity emphasizes that immigrant churches are best viewed as adapting organizations. The basic assumption of this approach is that the assimilation process invariably transforms an ethnic group over the course of several generations. Organizational survival, therefore, will eventually require adapting to the acculturated generations. In the Social Sources of Denominationalism, Niebuhr provides the classic expression of this position.

Niebuhr's analysis is rooted in the recognition that immigrant churches tend to be conservative and, during their early stage of development, are "primarily conflict societies, intent upon maintaining their distinction from other groups" (1957:224).[5] Nevertheless, the history of immigrant churches reveals that the tendency toward conformity is ultimately the dominant force shaping their character. The process of assimilation forces the churches to choose between accommodation and extinction. As the second and third generations are raised in the new environment, the language and culture of the old world becomes increasingly unfamiliar and foreign. This inevitably leads to generational conflict over which language should be used in religious and social activities.

Progressive leaders maintain that the adoption of
English is essential for the successful incorporation of
the younger generations. Conservatives, on the other
hand, resist the language shift since it represents "the
abandonment of all the ways of the fathers."[6] The hard
reality of the progressive position is usually
grudgingly accepted in the end. "Though churches may
delay the moment of their surrender," Niebuhr remarks,
"few elect to perish with their mother tongue"
(1957:212).

Contemporary sociologists have also maintained
that the survival and growth of ethnic churches requires
organizational adaptations. In his study of ethnic
groups in Southern Alberta, Palmer (1972:239-245)
discovered a general pattern of accommodation in various
immigrant churches in their efforts "to stem the
defection of the second and third generations."
Similarly, in the United States Steinberg (1981:67-68)
points out that "ethnic subsocieties must adapt to the
prevailing culture to curtail the loss of more
assimilated members." Fishman (1972:621) also supports
this view observing that "the more 'successful' religion
becomes, the more de-ethnicized it becomes."[7]

These two perspectives on religion and ethnicity
correspond closely to the popular contrasting images of
the nature of society in Canada and the United States:
the "ethnic mosaic" and the "melting pot." These
images, or "rhetorical idealizations" (Simpson,
1977:18), imply that the assimilation of immigrants
proceeds in dissimilar patterns in these two countries.
Ethnic minorities in the United States are expected to
abandon their distinctive features and conform to
"Anglo-Saxon" culture (Herberg, 1961:21), whereas in

Canada they are both able and encouraged to maintain their cultural distinctiveness indefinitely.[8]

   The foundation for Canada's ethnic mosaic is, presumably, the biculturalism of its charter groups. This image of Canada has flourished over the past decade with the federal government's new policy on multiculturalism. Anderson and Frideres suggest that:

> Ethnic persistence has doubtless been encouraged in Canada by a general (if new) emphasis on toleration of multiculturalism as an ideology or goal. In other words, in a majority-minority situation, ethnic persistence will be enhanced if the majority does in fact accept the minority's right to distinctiveness (1981:107).

There are sociologists dissenting from this popular understanding of Canadian society. Dahlie and Fernado, for example, argue that in spite of the policy of multiculturalism and the existence of two charter groups with distinctive cultures, the pressure towards "Angloconformity" is also a dominant social reality of Canada:

> Although the locus of power has always been with the "charter groups" (vis-à-vis all other incoming groups) the relationship between the two has been asymmetrical with the "British" dominant and the "French" disadvantaged. An important consequence of British dominance is that Angloceltic institutions and ways of thinking have come to constitute the major components of Canadian norms, the ethos which "Other" ethnic groups, including the original habitants of this

land, are supposed to assume in the process
of becoming truly Canadian (1981:1).

Does Canada provide an environment in which ethnic
minorities can maintain their cultural distinctiveness
or is Anglo-conformity expected to accompany integration
into the host society? This case study of the Japanese
experience should provide some clarification of this
issue.

According to Gordon (1964:37), the persistence of
ethnicity or the "sense of peoplehood" depends to a
large degree upon the development of a subsociety; that
is, a network of ethnic organizations, informal social
relationships and institutional activities. In this
study, minority churches are regarded as key components
of the Japanese subsociety in Canada. These religious
organizations are the "plausibility structures" (Berger,
1969:45) or "base-institutions" (Shimpo, 1981:20) upon
which the maintenance of the Japanese subculture largely
depends.

From the foregoing discussion emerge two central
questions that provide the orientation for the remainder
of this study:

(1)   Are Japanese minority churches effective
      agents of cultural preservation in
      Canadian society? or

(2)   Does the assimilation process force
      Japanese   minority   churches   to
      de-ethnicize and accommodate to the
      acculturated generations for organiza-
      tional survival?

The following pages will attempt to provide empirically grounded answers to these questions.

The Typological Framework

The significance of Millett's sub-typology for the study of Japanese minority churches will be elaborated in relation to these two general perspectives on religion and ethnicity. In considering the further potential of this typology, I have shifted the focus away from the problem addressed by Mehl and Millett, that is, whether or not minority churches maintain their church-like character or become sectarian, to examine the issues of ethnic persistence and organizational adaptation. Millett's sub-typology draws attention to important differences between minority churches which could elucidate their effectiveness as social bases for ethnic persistence and/or their ability to make organizational adaptations for acculturated generations.

This comparative study of the foreign-oriented Buddhist Churches of Canada (hereafter the BCC) and the native-oriented Japanese United Church Conference (hereafter the JUCC) is based upon observed differences in the general orientation of their founding members and the character of the sponsoring religious body or administrative reference group. As far as the membership orientation is concerned, it is commonly recognized that for most Japanese immigrants in Canada the Buddhist churches symbolized Japanese culture and ties to the old country, whereas the Christian churches were viewed as hakujin (Caucasian) religion (Young and Reid, 1938:95-107; Shimpo, 1977:122-23). According to the "definitions of the situation" in the Japanese community, therefore, those affiliating with the

Buddhist churches tended to be more conservative and supporters of Japanese traditions. Conversion to one of the Christian churches, on the other hand, was interpreted as a movement into Anglo-society and an indicator of an assimilationist orientation.

The general orientation of the founding members of these two minority churches is closely connected to the character of the sponsoring religious bodies. The religious authority and legitimacy of the BCC is based upon its relationship to the Mother Temple of Jodo Shinshu (True Pure Land Sect), the Nishi Honganji in Kyoto, Japan. This organizational link with the old country reinforces the traditionalism of the BCC membership. Having a Mother Temple in Japan encourages the preservation of the ethnic language and culture in the BCC. This administrative reference group tends to be conservative and resistant to adaptations which would diminish its power and the dependence of the immigrant churches.

The sponsoring religious body of the JUCC is the United Church of Canada. The organizational relationship to an indigenous church reinforces the assimilationist orientation of the JUCC membership. According to the earlier administrators of the United Church, these ethnic congregations were viewed primarily as a stepping stone to full integration in the Anglo-Saxon community (MacDonald, 1951:53-54). For this indigenous sponsoring religious body, therefore, the Christianization process was inseparable from the process of Canadianization (Clifford, 1977:24).

With these basic differences in mind, we will trace the development of the BCC and JUCC and compare their effectiveness as "plausibility structures"

(Berger, 1969:45) for ethnic persistence. In exploring the assimilationist perspective, we will analyze the ability of these two minority church organizations to make adaptations for the acculturated generations.

A basic assumption underlying this study is that minority church evolution cannot be understood apart from a knowledge of the socio-cultural changes within the larger Japanese Canadian community. To provide this necessary context, the following chapter briefly sketches the history of the Japanese in Canada.

REFERENCES

1.   Wilson's (1959) early work provided one of the most important contributions to the sociology of sectarianism.   He challenged Niebuhr's (1957:19-20) widely known thesis that sectarian movements are inevitably transformed into church-type organizations after one generation.   Through an analysis of a variety of sects Wilson was able to isolate a number of factors in the organization and environment of sects which promote or retard this type of development. According to Wilson, key variables influencing the path of sect evolution are the nature of the host society (whether feudalistic, totalitarian, or democratic), the character of the sect ideology (based upon the sect's definition of mission), and the use of insulating and isolating mechanisms. Taking these factors into consideration, Wilson introduced a sub-typology of sects useful in determining which sects were the most likely candidates to follow the course of development outlined by Niebuhr.

2.   Mehl (1970:257) observes that: "The minority church considers the international community to which it is spiritually connected to be a sort of reference group, whose extensiveness, power, and universality helps keep the minority church from becoming a sect, from feeling itself to be a sect, from sectarian behavior."

3.   Following Mehl's line of thought, Millett also emphasizes the role of the parent church as a reference group preventing sectarian behavior. Minority church members are distinguished from sectarians "by their willingness to gradually accommodate to the religious behavior of the English speaking majorities" (1969:113). One could say that temporary language and cultural differences, rather than sectarian ideology, separate minority churches from the larger society.

4.   The lack of adequate studies analyzing religio-ethnic behavior through successive generations has been well-noted (See Gordon, 1964:199; Crispino, 1980:3; Kayal, 1973:409).

5.   Because of this preoccupation with the preservation of old world cultures, Niebuhr referred disparagingly to this social form of religion as "racial sectarianism." It should be remembered that as a theologian Niebuhr's central concern was ethical not sociological. For him,

sects, denominations, and immigrant churches represented the moral failure of Christianity since they sanctioned divisiveness and a "religion of the caste system" (1957:6). What social form "authentic" Christianity would take is not made entirely clear by Niebuhr (see, 1957:281-84).

6.   Niebuhr suggests that the intuitions of the conservatives have usually been correct "for the adoption of the native tongue is only the most obvious symptom of the assimilation of the native culture as a whole" (1957:212).

7.   Other sociologists have also recognized the need for ethnic organizations to adapt to the needs of the acculturated generations. See, for example, John E. Hofman, "The Language Transitions in Some Lutheran Denominations," in Joshua A. Fishman, ed. Readings in the Sociology of Language (The Hague: Mouton, 1968, 1972 Second Edition); and Baha Abu-Laban, "The Canadian Muslim Community: The Need for a New Survival Strategy," in Earle H. Waugh, Baha Abu-Laban, and Regula B. Qureshi, The Muslim Community in North America (Edmonton: The University of Alberta Press, 1983).

8.   Herberg pointed out some years ago that the process of assimilation in the United States is not accurately represented by the "melting pot" metaphor. The American's image of himself is not just a synthesis of various ethnic elements. The United States, he suggested, is in reality a "transmuting pot" in which various ethnic groups are "transformed and assimilated to an idealized 'Anglo-Saxon' model" (1960:21). Herberg recognized that the British cultural heritage constituted the primary influence upon ethnic minorities during their assimilation into American society.

CHAPTER TWO: RELIGION AND ASSIMILATION: THE JAPANESE EXPERIENCE IN CANADA

Introduction

Over the past century the circumstances of the Japanese in Canada have changed in remarkable ways. One indicator of this is the diverse way in which the Japanese have been regarded by the host society. During the course of their history in Canada they have been seen as much needed "cheap labor," as the "yellow peril," as "enemy aliens," and finally, as a "model minority." These different labels point to important transformations that have occurred in the social conditions of Japanese life in Canada. Apart from a knowledge of this changing social environment, an accurate understanding of minority church evolution cannot be attained. A historical perspective is indispensable for determining those conditions encouraging minority church persistence and those contributing to minority church decline and dissolution. In order to provide this necessary context, this chapter will briefly review the experience of the Japanese in Canada, focusing on the nature and extent of their assimilation.[1]

A particular concern of this chapter is to describe the major religious developments within the Japanese Canadian community. Millett (1979:183) has suggested that as immigrants settle in the New World at least four forms of religious adaptation usually occur: (1) secular assimilation (the abandonment of religion); (2) religious assimilation (the integration of immigrants into the existing religious institutions of the dominant group); (3) linguistic diversification (the

organization   of ethnic language congregations sponsored
by the indigenous churches of the dominant group, i.e.,
native-oriented minority churches); and (4) new formal
organizations (the establishment by the immigrants of
their own religious traditions in the New World, i.e.,
foreign-oriented minority churches).   The degree to
which Japanese religious adaptations have followed these
four patterns will be analyzed in the following
discussion.

Historical Overview

     This survey of Japanese Canadian history utilizes
the framework elaborated by Shimpo (1977:30).   Shimpo
divides the history of Japanese Canadians into four
periods according to their changing legal status.   Since
the assimilation of minorities depends to a certain
extent upon their acceptance or rejection by the
dominant group, this framework is well-suited to our
purposes.   The process and limits of Japanese
assimilation in Canada during each period has been
determined by the attitudes and policies of those
wielding political power.   The first period, 1877-1907,
Shimpo describes as one of "free entry;" there were no
quotas on the number of Japanese immigrants permitted to
enter Canada for these first thirty years.   During the
second period, 1908-1940, the number of Japanese allowed
to enter Canada was limited and various aspects of
Japanese economic activity and employment were
restricted by the government.   The third period, 1941-
1949, begins with the severing of diplomatic relations
between Japan and Canada.   Throughout this period
Japanese immigrants and their Canadian-born children
were regarded as enemy aliens and denied their rights as
citizens.   In the last period, 1950 to the present,

Japanese Canadians finally received full legal status and rights as citizens of Canada.

With Dreams of Riches: 1877-1907

The first phase of Japanese immigration to Canada began in the late nineteenth century and was comprised primarily of men who had come to meet the demand for manual laborers in the developing industries of British Columbia. The internal causes for this movement have been related to the rapidly increasing population and its attendant economic pressures, especially among the peasant class from the districts of southern Japan (Yoshida, 1901:384). Many of those who came to Canada intended to return to Japan after a few years of diligent labor with enough capital to purchase their own farms or establish businesses. For most Japanese immigrants this dream never materialized.

The economic activities of the early Japanese immigrants were concentrated in fishing, lumbering, railroading, and mining. While those in control of the developing industries of British Columbia encouraged laborers to come from Japan, they had no interest in the Japanese becoming full participants in Canadian life. To insure that Anglos maintained control of the province, the legislature of British Columbia denied the vote to the Japanese in 1895.

The increasing number of Japanese arriving in British Columbia was accompanied by growing anti-oriental sentiments. To the white working class the Japanese represented cheap labor and unfair competition. The hostility towards orientals culminated in 1907 when the Asiatic Exclusion League held a rally in Vancouver.

The rally was effective and a riot ensued, with a white
mob storming the Japanese Powell Street community and
China Town. As a result of this conflict, the Japanese
and Canadian governments negotiated a "Gentlemen's
Agreement" to restrict the number of Japanese permitted
to enter Canada, and announced it the following year
(Shimpo, 1977:73).

The assimilation of the Japanese during this first
period of settlement in Canada was extremely limited.
One important factor discouraging their assimilation was
their rejection by the Caucasian community. Due to
their experience of prejudice and discrimination, the
Japanese tended to labor together in groups and live in
segregated communities. In addition to the outside
hostility of the host society, the language and cultural
differences of the Japanese also encouraged the
development of a distinct subsociety. In Vancouver a
section of town known as "Little Tokyo" grew rapidly and
became the centre of the Japanese community. By the end
of this first period, the Japanese ghetto consisted of
thirty-two restaurants, twenty-six boarding houses, and
two Japanese religious institutions (Shimpo, 1977:51).
Christian missionary efforts among the Japanese
immigrants in British Columbia were initiated during
this period. Together, the Methodists and Anglicans had
several missions offering religious services and
instruction in the English language. In spite of these
efforts, cultural assimilation was not significant
during these early years.

The Family Building Phase: 1908-1940

As a result of the "Gentlemen's Agreement," in
1908 the Japanese government began issuing passports and

restricted the number of Japanese male laborers entering
Canada to four hundred per year. The consequences of
this new policy and the hostile political climate was
the drastic decline in Japanese immigration to Canada,
from a high of over 7,000 during 1907-1908 to only 244
the following year (Adachi, 1976: Appendix 1). Excluded
from this restriction, however, were returning residents
and relatives of those Japanese already in Canada
(Shimpo, 1977:73). The composition of the Japanese
population changed considerably as male laborers sent
for "picture brides" and family members in Japan. In
the Japanese Canadian community, Adachi (1976:87)
observes, "1908 marked the beginning of the 'family-
building' phase." Between 1901 and 1941 the percentage
of Canadian-born Japanese increased from 1.4 to 59.1
percent (Shimpo, 1977:150).

The economic activities of the Japanese during
this second period continued to be shaped by racial
discrimination and increasing government restrictions.
In the fishing industry, for example, the government
began cutting back the number of fishing licenses issued
to the Japanese due to the growing animosity and
pressure from occidental workers. Because of these
discriminatory practices, the number of Japanese
involved in fishing declined from 2,933 to 1,998, or
31.8 percent, between 1922 and 1932 (Shimpo, 1977:81).
Similar practices also contributed to the decline of the
number of Japanese involved in railroad, mining, and
lumbering during the same decade. Restrictions in these
areas encouraged the Japanese to pursue more independent
economic ventures in agriculture and commerce. The
increase in Japanese businesses was particularly evident
in Vancouver where by 1931 they held over eight hundred
trading licenses. "There was one license for every ten

Japanese in the city," Adachi (1976:151) notes, "to only one for every twenty-one non-oriental."

The exclusionary practices of the host society encouraged the continued development of a separate Japanese community. In this unfavorable environment the Japanese maintained a relatively segregated society. By 1941 approximately 96 percent of the 23,149 Japanese in Canada were in British Columbia, and about three-fourths of them were concentrated within seventy-five miles of Vancouver (Adachi, 1978:6). During this second period the Japanese subsociety was characterized by a high degree of "institutional completeness" (Breton, 1964). A network of Japanese prefectural associations, religious institutions, businesses, newspapers, and schools developed and limited the degree of contact between Japanese and Caucasians, thereby discouraging assimilation.

The organization of Japanese language schools was a central concern of this period. The first Japanese language school was established in 1906. By 1940 there were 48 language schools with 4,012 students and 97 teachers in the Japanese communities across British Columbia (Shimpo, 1977:105). The Issei (first generation) sought to establish language schools for two main reasons. First, since Issei were generally unable to speak or understand English, intergenerational communication would only be possible if the Nisei (second generation) learned Japanese. Second, some Issei still had intentions of returning to Japan with their families and they knew that their children would have to be fluent in Japanese if they were to survive upon their return (Shimpo, 1977:105-6). Those Nisei forced by their parents to attend Japanese school were later to find their language ability to be a great

asset; as they were subsequently excluded from full
employment in the Caucasian community, Nisei found that
they needed Japanese language ability in order to work
in the Issei dominated subculture (Sunahara, 1979:2).

The exclusionary practices of the dominant group
kept many Japanese isolated. Nevertheless, significant
links with Anglo-society for the second generation led
to a considerable degree of cultural assimilation. The
most important acculturative force upon the Nisei during
this period was the public school. As Table II-1 shows,
a substantial number of Canadian-born Japanese were
enrolled in the public school system during this period.
The second generation, therefore, were socialized in two
vastly different social worlds: the Japanese world of
their parents, and the Anglo world of their Caucasian
peers. At home and in the ethnic language schools the
Nisei were inculcated with the traditional Japanese
value of social conformity. Upon entering the public
schools they were faced with other cultural values,
encouraging them to assert their individuality
(Maykovich, 1972:58). It was inevitable that
intergenerational conflict would occur as the Caucasian
community became an increasingly important reference
group for the second generation.

Another important acculturative force upon the
Japanese in Canada was the missionary activity of
several Christian denominations. Although the Japanese
immigrants were predominantly Buddhist, their
evangelistic efforts met with considerable success. The
most serious attempts to evangelize the Japanese were
carried out by the United and Anglican Churches (Mitsui,
1964; Nakayama, 1966:31). Before the Second World War,
their combined work consisted of thirteen missions in
British Columbia. On a smaller scale, missionary work

among the Japanese was also undertaken by the Roman
Catholic Church.

Table II-1

Second Generation Japanese Enrolled in Public
Schools of British Columbia, 1917-1940

YEAR	ELEMENTARY SCHOOL	HIGH SCHOOL	UNIVERSITY
1917	600	11	6
1922	1,422	--	--
1924	1,725	43	8
1925	2,477	--	--
1930	4,128	410	--
1935	5,405	697	--
1940	5,395	1,359	--

SOURCE: Shimpo, 1977:103.
NOTE: --Dash means no data available.

In addition to providing religious services, these
Christian churches organized English night schools to
assist the immigrants in their adjustment to the new
environment (Sumida, 1935:122, 132).   Special efforts
were made among the Canadian-born young people.   Sunday
schools and kindergartens were established, and various
Christian clubs were organized.   As a result of these
many efforts, scores of second-generation Japanese were
exposed to the Christian religion at some point during
their childhood.   In 1938 alone, for example, there were
1,161 Nisei enrolled in 18 Sunday schools and 834
involved in some 47 through-the-week organizations such
as Canadian Girls in Training and Mission Band.[2]   A 1934

survey of 10,774 Nisei in British Columbia indicates
that these efforts were not in vain; 43.6 percent
identified themselves with one of the Christian
denominations.[3]   Since Japanese view Christianity as
the religion of Canada, conversion to one of the
Christian denominations symbolized movement into Anglo
society and is therefore an indicator of cultural
assimilation (Shimpo, 1977:123).

Although the Japanese Buddhists were slower in
organizing their religious services in Canada, by the
mid-1930s there were six Buddhist Churches in British
Columbia and one as far east as Raymond, Alberta
(Kawamura, 1977:505). The Buddhist tradition, of
course, symbolized Japanese culture, and its
organization and activities in Canada provided a basis
for maintaining Japanese identity (Shimpo, 1977:122).
Representing familiar customs and values, the Buddhist
activities were especially attractive to the Issei.
Nevertheless, even among the first generation the
Christian denominations began to make an impact. By
1941, the foreign-born Japanese in Canada still
identifying themselves as Buddhist had declined to 69.7
percent.[4]

In summarizing the extent of assimilation during
this period, it could be said that the Issei largely
remained an unacculturated generational unit within the
Japanese community. While there were conversions to one
of the Christian denominations, most Issei remained
enclosed within the network of ethnic institutions and
relationships. For the Nisei, on the other hand,
cultural assimilation was quite advanced. In addition
to the religious changes already noted, the language
abilities of Canadian-born Japanese were rapidly
transformed through their exposure to the public school

system. A 1935 survey of 4,261 Nisei revealed that 41.5 percent could read English only, 44 percent could read both English and Japanese, and a mere 14.3 percent could read Japanese only. According to this study, most of those who could only read Japanese had been sent back to Japan for a significant portion of their education and then returned to Canada.[5]

In spite of their high degree of cultural assimilation, Nisei were denied free entry to the jobs for which their education had prepared them. Many businesses refused to employ Japanese Canadians because of the attitudes of many occidental workers. Even university educated Nisei were barred from government employment and the teaching profession (Sunahara, 1979:2). The prejudice and discriminatory practices of the dominant group meant that even though the Canadian-born Japanese were acculturated to Anglo society, structural assimilation would not occur for many years.

Life as Enemy Aliens: 1941-1949

With the severing of diplomatic relations between Japan and Canada in 1941, Japanese immigrants and their Canadian-born children faced further discriminatory actions. Under the direction of Prime Minister Mackenzie King, all Japanese in Canada were ordered to register with the government on January 8, 1941. Apparently, this was a racist policy to which Germans and Italians in Canada were not subjected. As a result of this order 1,950 Japanese Nationals (8.9 percent of Japanese in Canada) were issued yellow cards; 3,200 naturalized Japanese (14.5 percent of Japanese in Canada) were issued pink cards; and 16,860 Canadian-born Japanese (76.6 percent) were issued white cards (Shimpo, 1977:139).

The bombing of Pearl Harbor on December 7, 1941, marked the end of an era for the Japanese in Canada. Japanese immigrants and their children were immediately regarded as enemy aliens and the government began to impose restrictions under the authority of the War Measures Act (Barr, 1978:346). The Canadian government closed the 51 Japanese language schools in British Columbia, stopped publication of the three Japanese language newspapers, and confiscated 1,200 Japanese-owned fishing boats (Shimpo, 1977:140; Adachi, 1976:200).

More radical measures were yet to be implemented against the Japanese. Under "racist pressure" (Adachi, 1976:215) the government abandoned its initial plan for a selected evacuation of Japanese Nationals; it decided that all enemy aliens, including naturalized citizens and Canadian-born Japanese, would have to be removed from the "protected area"--a 100 mile strip of land along the coast of British Columbia--where most of the 23,149 Japanese were concentrated. The evacuation program was implemented by the British Columbia Security Commission, and completed by the end of October, 1942. After being temporarily housed in the livestock stalls of Vancouver's Hasting Park, the Japanese were assigned to several different projects. Many of the men were placed on federal road projects in the interior of British Columbia. Several thousand men and their families were sent to work on the sugar-beet farms of Alberta and Manitoba. The majority were assigned to relocation centres in the ghost towns of southeastern British Columbia (Violette, 1948:96; Shimpo, 1977:153).

The systematic removal of all the Japanese from the coastal areas of British Columbia irreversibly altered the social and economic structure of the Japanese

community. The evacuation meant, of course, the
disintegration of "Little Tokyo" in Vancouver as well as
other Japanese communities scattered in the coastal
area. The authority and leadership of the Issei, the
immigrants who had been the backbone of the pre-war
community economically, declined as they lost their
homes, stores, fishing boats, and farms (Sunahara,
1979:5-13). Upon orders of the federal government, the
Custodian of Enemy Property disposed of all Japanese-
owned property located within the "protected area." A
survey conducted by the Japanese Canadian Committee for
Democracy in 1947 indicated that the Japanese had
incurred a loss of 25 percent in the liquidation of
their property (Miyata, 1971).

In order to continue their missionary work among
the Japanese during the war years, the United, Anglican,
and Roman Catholic Churches reassigned their ministers
and lay workers to the various relocation centres
(Mitsui 1964:272; McWilliams, 1943). The churches
gained many new members through their efforts during the
war. In addition to religious outreach, a key factor
accounting for their success was the educational
programs they organized in the centres. The evacuation
had removed many Japanese young people from areas where
public education was available; therefore, where the
government did not provide assistance, the Christian
churches made every effort to set up "stopgap schools"
and kindergartens (Sunahara, 1981:87-97). For most high
school students this simply meant that the churches
provided tutors to supervise their correspondence
courses. Nevertheless, in many cases attendance at
church-sponsored classes was simply the prelude to
church attendance and membership in one of the major
denominations.[6] A comparison of the religious composition of Japanese Canadians in 1941 and 1951 reveals the

progress made by the Christian denominations. As indicated in Table II-2, those Japanese identifying themselves with one of the major Christian denominations increased from 30.5 percent to 56.7 percent during this ten year period.[7]

Table II-2

Japanese Population According to Percentage
Adhering to Each of the Four Principle
Denominations, 1941 and 1951

	1941		1951	
DENOMINATION	NUMBER	PERCENTAGE	NUMBER	PERCENTAGE
Buddhist	14,759	63.75	8,792	40.58
United Church	4,965	21.44	8,448	38.99
Anglican	1,653	7.14	2,933	13.50
Roman Catholic	450	1.94	921	4.25
TOTAL POPULATION	23,149		21,663	

SOURCE: Census of Canada, 1941 and 1951.

An important topic of discussion during the war was the future of the Japanese in Canada. Politicians, particularly those in British Columbia, frequently argued that extreme measures would be required to solve the Japanese problem. The virulent attitudes of many Caucasians is well-illustrated by the following statement of Liberal MP Thomas Reid on January 15, 1942:

Take them back to Japan. They do not belong here, and there is only one solution to the problem. They cannot be assimilated as Canadians for no matter how long the Japanese remain in Canada they will always be Japanese.[8]

This extreme position gained wide popular support and significantly influenced the federal government's decision regarding the future of the Japanese in Canada.

As the Second World War came to a close, the Canadian government informed the Japanese that they had two options: either cooperate with the policy of geographical dispersal and resettlement east of the Rockies, or be repatriated back to Japan. Almost 7,000 Japanese made application for repatriation to Japan, though not without considerable inter-generational conflict. Many Nisei resisted their parents decision to return to Japan because they identified themselves as Canadians and had an inadequate knowledge of the Japanese language (Barr, 1978:348; Shimpo, 1977:187). Of those who initially signed up for repatriation, only about 4,000 actually returned to Japan (Adachi, 1978:30).

As a result of the policy of geographical dispersal and resettlement, cities and towns in eastern Canada absorbed thousands of Japanese after the war. The success of this government policy is revealed in the fact that in 1941 over 95 percent of the Japanese were concentrated in British Columbia; a decade later, however, only 33 percent of the Japanese remained in this western province.

The policy of the Canadian government toward the Japanese during the war was considerably more severe than the treatment of the Japanese in the United States. Maykovich points out that "internment began earlier and ended later in Canada" (1975:103). Furthermore, the restrictions upon Japanese Canadians and their status as enemy aliens remained until 1949. In that year the Japanese were finally allowed to return to the coastal areas of British Columbia and granted equal citizenship rights by the Provincial Legislature (Adachi, 1976:344).

Home at Last?   1950 to Present

The war, evacuation, and resettlement brought about massive changes in the character of the Japanese community in Canada. In the prewar period the Japanese were a highly visible and segregated group with many of their own social and economic institutions. The evacuation and disposal of Japanese property effectively destroyed the ethnic subsociety which had developed for over half a century in British Columbia. Also, their dispersal across Canada since the war has significantly reduced their visibility. Consequently, racial discrimination has decreased and economic opportunities for the Japanese have increased as they have no longer been perceived as a threat by the white community (Barr, 1978:49). Since 1950 the Japanese Canadians have had for the first time in their history full legal rights as citizens. As the social and economic barriers to full participation in Canadian society have been gradually reduced by the dominant group, economic mobility has increased among the Japanese population, and their assimilation into Anglo society has been accelerated.

An indicator of cultural assimilation is the adoption of the religion of the host society. The 1971 Canadian Census shows that the pattern of Christianization which began early in the history of the Japanese in Canada has continued in the post-war environment. As may be seen in Table II-3, approximately half of the Japanese population identify themselves with one of the Christian denominations. The United Church claims 30 percent of the population, and the Anglican Church claims 10 percent, clearly indicating the lasting influence of their missionary endeavors. The 17 percent claiming "No Religion" appears unusually high when compared to the 4.3 percent average for Canada. Just over 90 percent of those claiming "No Religion" among Japanese are urban residents.[9]

Table II-3

Religious Affiliation of Japanese
in Canada, 1971

DENOMINATION	NUMBER	PERCENT
Anglican	3,955	10.60
Baptist	600	1.60
Greek Orthodox	75	.20
Jewish	--	--
Lutheran	175	.46
Mennonite/Hutterite	85	.22
Pentecostal	220	.59
Presbyterian	440	1.10
Roman Catholic	1,795	4.80
Salvation Army	50	.13
Ukranian Catholic	10	.02
United Church	11,455	30.70
Other	11,945	32.00
No Religion	6,445	17.20
TOTAL:	37,260	100.00

SOURCE: Census of Canada, 1971, Vol. 1, Table 18.

What is "hidden" within the religious categories of the Canadian Census, however, is a considerable amount of ethnic religious activity. There are at least 52 Japanese churches scattered across Canada. These

churches are located primarily in those provinces with
the largest concentration of Japanese, as indicated in
Table II-4. The size of these churches varies
considerably--from a small group of about 40 (Tenrikyo)
to a large congregation of 800 (Toronto Buddhist
Church). Most of these churches were organized during
the decade following the traumatic experience of the
evacuation and relocation. Many of the churches in
British Columbia, of course, are churches which existed
prior to the war; they were simply reorganized after
1949 when the government again permitted the Japanese to
settle in the coastal areas.

Table II-4

Distribution of Japanese Population in Canada and
Number of Ethnic Churches

PROVINCE	POPULATION	CHURCHES
Newfoundland	20	--
Prince Edward Island	15	--
Nova Scotia	85	--
New Brunswick	40	--
Quebec	1,745	4
Ontario	15,600	17
Manitoba	1,335	3
Saskatchewan	315	--
Alberta	4,460	11
British Columbia	13,585	17
Yukon	40	--
Northwest Territories	15	--
TOTAL	37,260	52

SOURCE: Census of Canada, 1971, and Church Reports.

Within the Japanese Canadian community both native-
oriented and foreign-oriented minority churches have

been well-established. As shown in Table II-5, almost
half of the churches are related to various Christian
traditions. The United Church with 11 congregations,
and the Anglican Church with 4 congregations, maintain
the most substantial native-oriented churches. The
Buddhist Churches of Canada with 18 congregations
remains the largest foreign-oriented religious
organization. While remaining quite small, some of the
"new" Japanese religions--Konko, Sei-Cho-No-Ie, and
Tenrikyo--have also been established in Canada.

Table II-5

Japanese Churches in Canada by Denomination

DENOMINATION	NUMBER
Anglican	4
Buddhist Churches of Canada (Jodo Shinshu)	18
Free Methodist	1
Gospel Churches (independent/evangelical)	5
Grace Church (independent/evangelical)	1
Konko Church	2
Nichiren Buddhist Church	1
Pentecostal	1
Presbyterian	1
Roman Catholic	1
Sei-Cho-No-Ie	1
Seventh Day Adventist	1
Tenrikyo	4
United Church	11
TOTAL	52

SOURCE: Interviews and Church Reports.

In addition to the religious accommodations made by
Japanese in Canada, the decline in the number of those

claiming Japanese as "mother tongue" (i.e., the language a person first learned in childhood and still understands) is another indicator of cultural assimilation. According to the Census of Canada, between 1941 and 1971 those claiming Japanese as mother tongue declined from 22,359 to 16,890. Although 45 percent of the Japanese Canadian population claim Japanese as mother tongue, 72 percent indicated that English is the language most often spoken at home.[10]

Although Census data on changes in religious identification and language use provides rough measures of the extent of assimilation, an accurate understanding of the nature of assimilation requires that generational distinctions be considered. The contemporary Japanese Canadian community is by no means one homogeneous group; rather, there are three major generational units within this community which makes separate treatment necessary in the analysis of assimilation.

Generational Profiles

The terms "Issei," "Nisei," and "Sansei" refer to three subgroups within the Japanese Canadian community whose life experiences have been extremely diverse. As Sunahara (1979:2) observes, these terms "have sociocultural referents as well as generational ones." Exposure to and participation in changing sociocultural environments has caused the Japanese to identify themselves as members of separate generational units. On the basis of generation location, Mannheim (1952:291) points out, one can determine the "probable" or "typical" modes of thought and behavior. Because of the unique historical experience of the Japanese in Canada these generational terms have special significance,

suggesting divergent patterns of assimilation within
this ethnic community.

The life experience of most Issei began with
socialization into the cultural norms and values of
rural Meiji Japan. It was during the Meiji era (1868-
1911) that the first wave of Japanese immigration to
Canada occurred. These immigrants brought with them the
values of traditional Japan and managed to
institutionalize them by establishing their own language
schools, prefectural associations, churches, and
businesses. These immigrants were "proud of their race
and culture" (Maykovich, 1972:36) and concerned that
their heritage be maintained in the New World.

The Nisei experience in Canada was more confusing
than that of their parents. At home and in the ethnic
community the Canadian-born Japanese were taught the
traditional Japanese values of their parents. Education
in the public school system taught them another language
and the values of individualism and self-expression.
Acculturated to Anglo society, yet excluded from free
entry and full participation, the Nisei were marginal
individuals unable to feel completely at home in either
the Japanese ghetto or the Caucasian community.

The Sansei have grown up in an altogether different
environment. While some were born in relocation centres
during the war, most were born during the resettlement
period. Consequently, they have never been exposed to a
tightly knit ethnic community as were their parents.
Neither have they had to experience the intense racism
and discrimination that was so much a part of Japanese
Canadian life for decades. The geographical dispersal
of the Japanese since the Second World War has meant
that most Sansei have been raised in Caucasian

neighborhoods and experienced very little of their life among a Japanese peer group.

These vastly different life experiences have shaped the generational patterns of assimilation within the Japanese Canadian community.   Useful data for the construction of generational profiles have been provided by two sociological studies of Japanese in Toronto conducted during the past decade (Makabe, 1976; Maykovich, 1980).[11]

The Issei are now an elderly sub-group within the contemporary Japanese community. If adoption of the language of the host society is regarded as a key indicator of cultural assimilation, this group is far from acculturated. Of Maykovich's sample of 48 Issei, "not a single respondent showed fluency in English" (1980:72). The lack of ability in English has meant that the nature of the relationships cultivated by members of this generation have been very limited. Although there is no longer an ethnic ghetto as such, Maykovich found that the friends of those in this sub-group "are predominantly other Issei" (1982:73).

Due to their education in the Canadian public schools, the cultural assimilation of Nisei is considerably more advanced. Maykovich discovered that all of the Nisei in her sample spoke English fluently. The efforts of Issei to transmit and maintain the Japanese language is reflected in the fact that 89 percent of the second generation attended language schools in British Columbia before the war. Maykovich found that one-quarter (24 percent) of the Nisei sample speak Japanese fairly well, one-fifth (21 percent) speak practically none, and one-half (55 percent) speak some Japanese (1980:76-77).

While Nisei are involved outside of the ethnic community in occupational associations and for employment, both Makabe (1976:174) and Maykovich (1980:77) found that they tended to prefer members of their own ethnic group for intimate friends. According to Maykovich (1980:77), 83 percent of the Nisei are likely to choose other Nisei as close friends. Makabe (1976:214) found that 55 percent of the Nisei men in her sample "did not include a single non-Japanese among their five intimates." In view of their traumatic history and harsh treatment by the Caucasian community for so many years, it is not surprising that they are most comfortable among their ethnic peers.

The Sansei represent a highly assimilated sub-group within the Japanese Canadian community. Raised in the post-war environment outside of the ethnic ghetto, Sanseispeak English fluently, but less than one-third speak some Japanese. The 9 percent able to speak Japanese fairly well, Maykovich (1980:78-79) points out, are mainly those few college students specializing in Japanese studies. The Caucasian sample in the Maykovich study were more concerned that Japanese parents transmit their ethnic heritage than were the Sansei.

Friendship patterns among Sansei are a good indicator of their integration into the Caucasian community. Maykovich (1980:70) found that "the majority of the Sansei have more non-Japanese (62 percent) than Japanese friends (38 percent)." Similar friendship patterns were discovered in Makabe's (1976:214) study. One important consequence of acceptance by the Caucasian community and new friendship patterns is the rapid increase in intermarriage among Sansei. In Makabe's study, 86 percent of the Sansei married outside of the ethnic community, exclusively to Caucasians. "Both married and non-married (Sansei respondents)," Makabe (1976:216) found, "agree with the idea that ethnic origin is not important in their choice of their spouses, and that they have no preference for ethnic endogamy at all." Toronto is not the only area of Japanese concentration where high rates of intermarriage among Sansei have been noted. Hirabayashi (1978:63-65) investigated the occurrence of intermarriage among Japanese Canadians in Southern Alberta and reported similarly high rates. In Lethbridge between 1970 and 1974, 82 percent of Japanese marriages were with non-Japanese. During the same period in the rural community of Taber the intermarriage rate was 71.4 percent. With intermarriage reaching such large proportions, it seems probable that both cultural and structural assimilation are nearly complete among the third generation Japanese.

Discussion

From the foregoing survey it is apparent that assimilation has progressed with each successive generation of Japanese in Canada. What makes the Japanese experience so interesting is the fact that they are a "visible minority" and were at one time considered unassimilable. What accounts for their rapid movement toward assimilation? It is certainly related to the unusual treatment of the Japanese by the Canadian government as a result of the Second World War; their evacuation and geographical dispersal transformed the nature of the ethnic community almost overnight. In the case of the Japanese, their ethnic ghettos were artificially and prematurely dismantled and their mobility forced.

It could also be reasoned that the unique achievement motivation of the Japanese (Bellah, 1957:3;

DeVos, 1973:23, 173-4), analogous to the Protestant work ethic, has encouraged education, socio-economic advancement, and, as an unintended consequence, assimilation.[12] Montero (1981), in his study of the Japanese in the United States, has shown that the concommitant of upward mobility is outward mobility and the loosening of the bonds of the ethnic community.

Finally, the racism and discriminatory practices of the dominant group have declined significantly during the postwar period. The decline in discriminatory practices is, of course, closely related to the labour shortage economy of Canada following the Second World War.[13] Not only was the Canadian economy able to accommodate the Japanese minority group, it was also able to absorb "over 800,000 post-war immigrant workers between 1946 and 1961" (Richmond, 1961:69).

Using the objective indicators of language maintenance and endogamy, "ethnicity" is clearly a declining phenomenon as far as the Japanese Canadian community is concerned. This is hardly surprising since the experience of many minorities follows a similar pattern. Reflecting upon the experience of ethnic minorities in Canada, DeVries and Vallee (1980:171) explain that:

> Unless these minorities are regularly supple-
> mented by large numbers of entrants from
> elsewhere (that is, through sustained flows of
> immigrants into the country), or unless they
> establish fairly high degrees of segregation
> from the English parts of North American
> society (as do the Native Indians and Inuit,
> the French in Quebec, and the Mennonites and
> Hutterites in western Canada), they will

eventually be absorbed into an English North
American society, in which the only remnants
of the original cultural mosaic may well be
such things as folk dancing groups, choral
societies and various types of handicraft.
**Strong countervailing forces must be developed
and cultivated to enhance the chances of
survival for such minorities.** (Emphasis mine)

Since the Second World War, the Japanese Canadian
community has neither been segregated from Anglo society
nor "regularly supplemented by large members of entrants
from elsewhere." In fact, between 1946 and 1976 only
10,332 Japanese immigrated to Canada and some of these
returned to Japan or moved to the United States (Ueda,
1978:21). As DeVries and Vallee pointed out above,
apart from segregation and/or significant replenishment
from abroad the survival of minorities requires the
development of "strong countervailing forces."

As noted in Chapter One, ethnic religious organizations are often regarded as central agents of cultural
preservation. The two largest religious organizations
within the Japanese Canadian community are the foreign-
oriented Buddhist Churches of Canada and the native-
oriented Japanese Conference of the United Church of
Canada. Are these minority churches effective
"countervailing forces" for the preservation of the
Japanese subculture? Has organizational survival
required adaptation or accommodation to the acculturated
second and third generations? What are the consequences
of the advancing structural assimilation for these
minority churches? In order to answer these questions,
the remainder of this study examines the development and
role of the BCC and JUCC in the Japanese Canadian
community.

REFERENCES

1.   Since Niebuhr's study of the consequences of "homogenization" (or "Americanization") upon immigrant church development, the conceptualization of the assimilation process has undergone considerable refinement. This study utilizes the framework advanced by Gordon (1964) in which seven distinct sub-processes or variables of assimilation are distinguished. Two of these sub-processes are of particular importance. According to Gordon, cultural assimilation (or acculturation) is usually the first type of assimilation to occur and involves a "change on the part of the ethnic group to the cultural patterns of the host society." Structural assimilation, the second process, involves "large-scale entrance into the cliques, clubs, and institutions of the host society, on the primary group level." Once structural assimilation occurs, Gordon maintains, the other types of assimilation usually follow. Full participation in the institutions of the host society naturally leads to marital assimilation (exogamy), identificational assimilation (the development of a sense of peoplehood based exclusively on the host society), attitude receptional assimilation (absence of prejudice), behavior receptional assimilation (absence of discrimination), and civic assimilation (absence of value and power conflict). In terms of Gordon's (1964:70-75) model of assimilation, this study of minority church adaptation is concerned with the organizational dilemmas posed particularly by cultural assimilation, structural assimilation, and marital assimilation.

2.   Reported in The Japanese Contribution to Canada: A Summary of the Role Played by the Japanese in the Development of the Canadian Commonwealth (Vancouver: Canadian Japanese Association, 1940): 31; University of British Columbia Special Collections, Japanese Collection.

3.   Report of the Survey of Second Generation Japanese in British Columbia (Vancouver: Canadian Japanese Association, 1935): 35; University of British Columbia Special Collections, Japanese Collection. It should be noted that in this survey "small children who were too young to belong to any religious organization were given the religious denomination of their parent or the same denomination as older children" (1935:35). It is interesting to note that even in this early period the

number of those identifying themselves with "no
religion" was already quite high. This survey found that
10.3 percent of the second generation "definitely
expressed the non-possession of any religious
connections or sentiments."

4.   Dominion Bureau of Statistics, Religious Denominations in Canada 1971-1941, Ottawa: 1947.

5.   Report of the Survey of the Second Generation
Japanese in British Columbia, ibid., p. 40.

6.   This observation is based upon interviews and
discussions with a number of Nisei members of various
Japanese United Churches.

7.   In addition to the active missionary work
conducted by the various Christian denominations,
another factor is probably related to the decline in the
Buddhist population during this period.   Since Japanese
Buddhists tended to be more conservative and least
oriented toward integration into Anglo society, they
were probably over-represented in the number of those
repatriated to Japan at the end of the Second World War
(Young and Reid, 1938:99-100; Shimpo, 1977:122).

8.   Quoted in 1977-1977 The Japanese Canadians: A
Dream of Riches (Vancouver: Japanese Canadian
Centennial Project, 1978): 77.

9.   The 1981 Canadian Census data on religion has not
yet been made available to the public.   Mr. Bob Stewart,
Archivist at Vancouver School of Theology, had an
opportunity to examine the unpublished reports and
informed me that the "No Religion" category among the
Japanese in 1981 had increased to 27.7 percent, the
average for Canada being 7.3 percent.

10.   1971 Census of Canada, 92-725, Vol.1, Part 3,
Tables 17 and 26.

11.   In Maykovich's (1980:72) study, the response rate
of 42 percent included 48 Issei, 100 Nisei, and 102
Sansei; for comparative purposes 103 Caucasians of
"approximately the same age and education levels as the
Sansei" were selected.   Makabe's (1976) study focused
upon Canadian-born Japanese in Toronto and was based
upon a sample of 100 Nisei and 20 Sansei.

12.   Economic mobility among second-generation Japanese
in Canada has been phenomenal. "In 1935 less than 1
percent of Japanese were professionals. . . . By 1974, a
sample of Toronto Nisei had an average family income of
$23,167.00 annually, almost twice the Canadian average"
(Baar, 1978:349-50).

13.   Richmond (1961:42) explains that "because of low
birthrates of the inter-war period, the additions to the
labour force by natural increase were insufficient to
meet the needs of a rapidly expanding economy in the
first decade after the war and immigration played a
vital part in sustaining economic growth."

CHAPTER THREE: FOREIGN-ORIENTED
MINORITY CHURCHES

Introduction

Foreign-oriented minority churches are ethnic religious organizations which operate in a non-official language and are dependent upon a parent organization overseas for leadership and authority in religious matters. Linked to a mother church in the old country, the primary administrative reference group of these churches is outside of Canada. The Buddhist Churches of Canada represent the largest foreign-oriented minority church organization within the Japanese Canadian community. Since the Japanese immigrants were dominantly Buddhist, it was almost assured that some form of Buddhist association would develop over the course of their settlement in Canada. In Japan, these immigrants had been affiliated with various Buddhist sects or schools. After their arrival in Canada, however, it was the Nishi Honganji, one of the two Jodo Shinshu (True Pure Land) schools, which responded to their religious needs (Kawamura, 1977:41). As a result, it has been the True Pure Land Buddhism which has been most effectively established among Japanese in Canada.

Historical Development

The origins of the Buddhist Churches of Canada can be traced to the informal gatherings of Japanese immigrants around the turn of the century. As early as 1901, Japanese were meeting regularly for "Dharma Talks" in the home of a dedicated Buddhist layman near New Westminister, British Columbia (Izumi, 1983:2). Within this initial association of Buddhist immigrants there arose an apprehension regarding the evangelistic efforts of various Christian denominations. According to one account, the progress of these Christian missions among the Japanese immigrants served as an impetus for Buddhists to become more formally organized (Ikuta, 1981:16).

In November 1904, a small group of Japanese met to discuss the possibility of establishing a Buddhist organization in Vancouver. By the end of this meeting two important decisions had been made: one was to form a religious body under the name Nihon Bukkyo Kai (Japanese Buddhist Church or Association), and the other was to petition Nishi Honganji, the Mother Temple of one of the Jodo Shinshu schools in Kyoto, Japan, to send a Buddhist priest to provide religious services in Vancouver. The Mother Temple responded favorably to this petition, and the first Buddhist missionary arrived the following year (Ikuta, 1981:17; Tsunemitsu, 1964:308).

During the priest's first year of residence in Vancouver, religious services were conducted in rented facilities. By 1906, the priest and a building committee of Nihon Bukkyo Kai had raised enough funds from sympathetic Japanese in Vancouver and the surrounding communities to purchase several lots of land and a house on Alexander Street. In addition to holding weekly religious services, an English night school and a Young Adult Buddhist Association (Bukkyo Seinen Kai) were organized by the priest in these new quarters. The religious and social activities of the Buddhist Church held considerable attraction for many immigrants who were not yet fully at home in their new environment. Within a few years the membership of the Nihon Bukkyo Kai grew to approximately 650 (Izumi, 1983:3; Shimpo,

1977:122). In 1909, this first Buddhist organization in Canada was incorporated under the laws of British Columbia and officially recognized by the Provincial government (Tsunemitsu, 1964:309).

The demographic changes occurring within the Japanese Canadian community as a result of the "Gentlemen's Agreement" encouraged other developments within the Vancouver Buddhist Church. After 1908, the number of Japanese women entering Canada increased significantly. Many of these women were quickly drawn into the life of the Buddhist Church. In 1913, a chapter of the Buddhist Women's Association was organized in Vancouver, and approximately one hundred women attended the inaugural meeting (Ikuta, 1981:29).

In 1920, the Vancouver Buddhist Church faced its first major crisis. The membership split into two factions with the dissenting group accusing the minister of inappropriate use of funds. This group left to organize a new church on Jackson Avenue. The leadership of this new group named its organization Canada Bukkyo Kai (Canada Buddhist Church or Association) and immediately petitioned the Mother Temple in Kyoto to send another priest. Within a short time, Nishi Honganji sent a priest to provide leadership for this new Buddhist organization. Under the leadership of this new priest the first Buddhist Sunday school was established in Canada. The leaders of the Bukkyo Kai began to realize that the future of Buddhism depended upon an effective program of religious socialization for the growing families in the Japanese community (Ikuta, 1981:35).

Four years after the schism, the Mother Temple sent another priest to Vancouver with the difficult assignment of reconciling the two Buddhist factions. The priest interviewed representatives from both sides and was finally able to negotiate a joint meeting to discuss reunion. The meeting proved successful, and the two Buddhist groups were reconciled in 1924 under the new name Honpa Canada Bukkyo Kai (Ikuta, 1981:42-45).

Although Vancouver was the centre of Buddhist activities during this early period, Buddhist groups were also being organized in other communities where Japanese were settling in significant numbers. As in Vancouver, most of these groups began as informal gatherings in homes with occasional visits from the priest of the Vancouver Buddhist Church. By 1930, there were Buddhist churches established in New Westminster, Marpole, Steveston, and Mission, British Columbia, and one as far east as Raymond, Alberta.

The growth of these churches was accompanied by a concern for greater organizational independence. During the first three decades of Buddhism in Canada, these churches were regarded as part of the North American Buddhist Mission which had its headquarters in the United States. In February of 1931, priests and lay delegates from the various churches in Canada met to consider separating from this umbrella organization. As a result of this meeting, the leadership of these churches petitioned Nishi Honganji regarding their desire to become an independent missionary district with headquarters in Canada. The Mother Temple approved this request and the following year these churches formally separated from the Buddhist Mission of North America and became the Buddhist Mission of Canada (Ikuta, 1981:61).[1]

The steady progress of the Buddhist Mission of Canada over these first three decades may be seen in Table III-1.

Table III-1

Buddhist Churches and Membership in Canada, 1934

CHURCH	MEMBERSHIP
Honpa Canada, Vancouver	300
New Westminster	130
Royston	100
Fairview	180
Steveston	300
West Second Avenue	150
Marpole	40
Maple Ridge	100
Mission City	50
Kelowna	145
Chemainus	40
Raymond (Alberta)*	124
TOTAL	1,659

SOURCE: Young and Reid, 1938:96.
NOTE: *Statistics for Raymond are based upon the number
of individuals who pledged for the building of Raymond
Buddhist Church in 1930.

In 1934, there were 12 Buddhist groups established with
a total membership of over 1,500.   There were also six
priests to provide religious leadership for these
churches.   While the numbers involved are not
overwhelming, they represent a considerable increase in
organizational strength.

By 1940, the number of Buddhist Churches in Canada
had increased to 17 with eight priests providing religious leadership (Ikuta, 1981:91-93).   There were also
10 Buddhist Sunday schools by this time (Tsunemitsu,
1964:312).   According to one report, the membership of

these churches had grown to a total of 4,235.[2] The
reason behind this increase of over 2,500 members
between 1934 and 1940 is not entirely clear. It seems
probable that the statistics of 1934 were based only
upon adult supporters, whereas the statistics of 1940
included the number of children enrolled in the Buddhist
Sunday Schools, kindergartens, Young Buddhist
Associations, and perhaps language schools.

The Second World War had a profound impact upon the
development of the Buddhist Churches in Canada. The
federal government immediately prohibited these churches
from holding any special gatherings and regular
religious services. Priests were only permitted to
perform funeral services (Ikuta, 1981:85). Once the
Canadian government decided to evacuate all Japanese
from the "protected area," all of the churches within
this zone were closed and their property disposed of by
the British Columbia Security Commission. Only the
churches in Kelowna, British Columbia, and Raymond,
Alberta, were outside of this area and were allowed to
remain open through the war years. At the time of the
evacuation the Buddhist priests serving the churches in
the coastal areas of British Columbia were relocated
with the rest of the Japanese. During the war the eight
priests continued Buddhist services in the interior of
British Columbia and in Southern Alberta. Six priests
served the Japanese in the following locations: Tashme,
Slocan, Sandon, New Denver, Lemon Creek, and Kelowna
(British Columbia). Two priests served the growing
Japanese population in Picture Butte and Raymond,
Alberta, until the end of the war (Ikuta, 1981:94).

Since the centre of Buddhism before the war had
been in the Vancouver area, the government policy of
evacuation and resettlement east of the Rockies made it

necessary for Buddhist leaders to seriously plan for the future of Buddhism in Canada. In April 1946, some thirty representatives from the pre-war Buddhist churches met with four of the priests at Raymond Buddhist Church to discuss the reestablishment of Buddhism in Canada. Under the leadership of these priests, this group formed the Canada Bukkyo Fukyo Zaidan (An Economic Foundation for the Propagation of Buddhism in Canada). Raymond Buddhist Church was selected as the new national headquarters, and the committee began to publish a monthly newletter to keep the scattered Japanese informed of Buddhist activities. The leaders of this committee also encouraged Japanese Buddhists to reorganize churches in cities and towns where sufficient numbers resettled. Within a few years new churches were established in Coaldale, Taber, Lethbridge, Winnipeg, Toronto, Hamilton, and Montreal (Ikuta, 1981:111-12; Kawamura, 1977:496).

The major difficulty facing these new churches was the lack of trained religious leaders. This was not an entirely new problem. Between 1905 and 1942, for example, 18 priests had served in the various Buddhist Churches. On the average, priests spent less than four years in Canada, hardly enough time to become oriented to Canadian culture and fluent in the English language (Ikuta, 1981:87-90). At the end of the war this problem became critical. In 1946, the Canadian government ordered that the seven Japanese-born priests be deported. Five of the seven returned to Japan that year. The Japanese in Southern Alberta, with the support of Senator W.A. Buchanan, the editor of the Lethbridge Herald, signed a petition protesting the deportation orders. As a result of this protest, the two priests serving the Japanese Buddhists in Southern Alberta were permitted to remain in Canada.[3] The only

other Buddhist priest remaining in Canada was a
Canadian-born Japanese who had received religious
training in Japan just before the outbreak of the Second
World War; he moved east to Toronto to minister to the
Japanese as they resettled, and helped establish new
Buddhist Churches in Ontario and Quebec.

The Canada Bukkyo Fukyo Zaidan recognized their
desperate need for trained religious leaders, especially
priests who were Canadian-born and bilingual. Many of
the second generation Japanese in Canada were not fluent
in Japanese and it was clear that their children would
be even less able to understand Japanese. The Buddhist
churches needed priests who could communicate effectively with these increasingly acculturated generations.
In an effort to meet this need, two Canadian-born
Japanese were sent back to Japan for Buddhist training.
These two priests returned in 1950 to serve Buddhist
churches in Winnipeg and Southern Alberta.[4]

Since Japanese were not permitted to move back
within the "protected area" until 1949, the reorganization of Buddhist churches in the coastal area of British
Columbia lagged a few years behind the formation of new
churches in eastern Canada. When the British Columbia
Buddhist Federation was organized in 1955, the Japanese
had reestablished churches in Kamloops, Vernon, Fraser
Valley, Steveston, Vancouver, and Kelowna (Izumi,
1983:7-8).

During the 1950s, two developments occurred within
these churches. One was that all of these churches came
to be known collectively as the Buddhist Churches of
Canada (BCC), replacing the earlier designation Buddhist
Mission of Canada. The other was the division of Canada
into four districts (Kyoku). This division was a

natural development since churches were geographically dispersed, but shared the religious services of an inadequate number of priests. Representatives from various churches in a district composed the Kyoku Board which coordinated the ministerial assignments. The four districts were British Columbia, Alberta, Manitoba, and the Eastern district (Ontario and Quebec).

In 1965, the priests from all four districts met to discuss organizational changes within the BCC. The ministerial association made two important decisions at this meeting: first, Toronto was selected as the new national headquarters of the BCC, and, second, it was resolved that the BCC "should have its own Bishop" (Kawamura, 1977:496-497). Prior to this time, the Canadian churches had been served by the Bishop of the Buddhist Churches of America. With the approval of Nishi Honganji, Rev. N. Ishiura became the first Bishop of the Buddhist Churches of Canada.

During this same year, the BCC experienced a major rift in one of its four districts. Until 1965, the Alberta Kyoku was the official governing body of the Buddhists in Alberta; it was the administrative link between individual churches and the national organiza-tion. At one of the regular Kyoku meetings, a number of delegates were dissatisfied with the manner in which business was being handled and left the meeting declaring that the Kyoku was dissolved (Kawamura, 1997:500).[5] Some of those who remained at this meeting became the steering committee which drew up a constitu-tion for a new Buddhist organization in Alberta named the Honpa Buddhist Church of Alberta. When the dust finally settled, this new Buddhist organization had affiliated churches in Raymond, Rosemary, and Lethbridge. The old Kyoku organization, revived as a result of opposition from the new Honpa group, had affiliated churches in Picture Butte, Taber, Coaldale, and Lethbridge.

The new Honpa Buddhist Church of Alberta was not recognized officially by the national organization (that is, the Board of the BCC), and therefore was not regarded as legitimate by the Nishi Honganji in Kyoto, Japan. When the Honpa churches applied for membership in the BCC, they were notified that application had to be made through the old Alberta Kyoku. This was an administrative procedure to which Honpa churches were not willing to submit since it required an admission on their part that the Alberta Kyoku was in fact the legitimate district organization and representative body of the BCC. Efforts to reconcile these two Buddhist factions in Alberta were unsuccessful for about fifteen years.

In the late 1970s, the Calgary Buddhist Church began sponsoring an annual Alberta Buddhist Conference aimed at reconciling these opposing groups. Since the Calgary Buddhist Church had not been involved in the earlier problems, it was regarded as neutral by the other churches in Alberta. Both Honpa and Kyoku churches were invited to participate in these annual meetings. The conference was supported by members of both groups who were in favor of reconciliation. As a result of these annual meetings, the Alberta Buddhist Federation was formed. The chief concern of this new organization was to facilitate cooperation between the Honpa and Kyoku churches. In an attempt to speed up this process, the Bishop of the BCC assigned two rotating ministers to the seven churches affiliated with the Honpa and Kyoku organizations. While the objective of this ministerial arrangement was to encourage the sense of interdependence between these two groups and decrease their feelings of alienation, one lay Buddhist confessed that "there would be less ill-feeling if the Bishop and the Alberta Buddhist Federation had moved more slowly."

In spite of these efforts, the Honpa and Kyoku churches have not been fully reconciled. The BCC Board recognized that the Honpa churches would never apply for membership through the Kyoku organization because of so much past conflict and resentment. In 1982, the Board changed the constitutional by-laws of the BCC so that individual churches could apply directly for membership without submitting their application through the district orgaization. The three Honpa churches made applications that year and were finally accepted as member churches of the BCC.[6] As may be seen in Table III-2, there are currently 18 churches in the BCC with a total membership of 3,185.

Religious Beliefs and Practices of the BCC

The Buddhist Churches of Canada belong to the Nishi Honganji, one of the two Jodo Shinshu schools (True Pure Land) of Japanese Buddhism. Although many Buddhist schools emphasize that enlightenment must be achieved through personal effort or self-power (jiriki), the True Pure Land school proclaims a path to salvation through other-power (tariki). According to this tradition, a Buddha named Amida (Infinite Light) will provide salvation: that is, rebirth in the Pure Land at death for all those who have faith in his goodness and accept his merit (DeBary, 1972:316; Cook, 1975:231).

Table III-2
Buddhist Churches of Canada Membership, 1983

CHURCH	MEMBERSHIP
District of British Columbia	
Kelowna	103
Fraser Valley	50
Kamloops	163
Steveston	452
Vernon*	6
Vancouver*	472
District of Alberta	
Calgary	150
Rosemary	22
Raymond	100
Taber	45
Coaldale	36
Lethbridge Honpa	225
Lethbridge Buddhist Association	190
Picture Butte*	35
District of Manitoba	
Manitoba Buddhist Association	190
Eastern District	
Toronto	800
Hamilton	66
Montreal	80
TOTAL	3,185

SOURCE: Organizational Questionnaire.
NOTE: *Statistics for Vernon and Vancouver are from the 1982 Annual Report, and those for Picture Butte were provided by Rev. Okada (Interview, 7 June 1983).

From the perspective of Pure Land Buddhism, this present age is one of confusion and degeneracy. The imperfections of this world and the basic requirements of daily life (such as, working for a living and caring for parents and children) prevent most individuals from following the disciplined religious practice required to achieve enlightenment in this life. It is for those who are unable to follow the path of self-effort that Amida Buddha established the Pure Land, a perfect environment where all beings can attain enlightenment. The only requirement for rebirth in the Pure Land is reciting the Nembutsu, "Namu Amida Butsu," which literally means "I rely on Amida Buddha." If the Nembutsu is recited with the mind of faith, rebirth in the Pure Land at death is assured.[7] The Bishop of the BCC summarized Pure Land Buddhist beliefs with the following confession of faith:

> I believe in the Amida Buddha who has established a Pure Land.
> I believe that the Jodo Shinshu teachings were taught by Shakyamuni Buddha in the three Sacred Scriptures of the Pure Land.
> I believe that our lives should be ones of gratitude to Amida and through that feeling of gratitude we should follow the eightfold path and the four noble truths.
> These are the cardinal beliefs.

It is interesting to note that the form of Buddhism institutionalized in Canada is the tradition which on the popular level is most similar to Christianity. A central affirmation of the Christian religion has always been that personal salvation is based upon faith in Jesus Christ (other power).

In the North American environment, Buddhism has undergone some significant modifications.[8] The organization of Sunday schools and regular Sunday services are clear departures from the normal practice of Buddhism in Japan. In Japan, except for special festivals and

holiday services, most rituals and ceremonies are
conducted before the Buddhist altar (butsudan) in the
home and without the assistance of a priest (Beardsley,
1959:448; Earhart, 1974:6, 126). More than the location
and occasion of services has been altered. Goa and
Coward (1983:373), in their study of the Raymond
Buddhist Church, point out that:

> Seventy-five years in Canada has changed Jodo
> Shinshu's use of sacred language from a
> uniquely Buddhistic form to a pattern more
> characteristic of Protestant Christianity. The
> sermon is stressed and the chant downplayed.

The shift from a family focus to a congregational
form of religion has not been entirely successful in
Canada. As may be seen in Table III-3, attendance at
regular Sunday services in most Buddhist churches is
generally low. There has always been, however, a
substantial turnout of members for those special
Buddhist services that are recognized in Japan. These
special religious days and services include:
Hanamatsuri and Nehan-e, commemorating the birth and
death of Shakyamuni Buddha; Gotan-e and Ho-onko,
commemorating the birth and death of Shinran Shonin, the
founder of the True Pure Land tradition in Japan. A
festival and service which is well-attended by both
members and numerous nominal Buddhists in the various
Japanese communities is the O-Bon. Observed in either
July or August, this day begins with a visit to the
cemetaries. The graves are cleaned and flowers and
incense are placed before them. Frequently, a Buddhist
priest conducts brief services for families at various
grave sites. The day concludes with a memorial service
at the church for all the deceased members of the church
families. In some of the larger Japanese communities in

Table III-3

Attendance at Regular and Special Services in the BCC, 1983

CHURCH (MEMBERSHIP)	REGULAR SERVICE	NEW YEARS	HO-ONKO	NEHAN-E	HANAMATSURI	GOTAN-E	OBON
Toronto (800)	100	175	175	150	600	175	700
Hamilton (66)	15	40	40	--	40	40	100
Montreal (80)	20	20	60	15	50	30	60
Manitoba (190)	35	60	60	35	100+	60	100+
Fraser Valley (50)	40	--	65	--	100	--	100
Kamloops (163)	30	50	60	--	70	60	80
Kelowna (103)	20	25	20	--	100	35	125
Steveston (452)	25	15	50	30	100	30	150
Vancouver (472)	125*	150	125	125	250	150	500
Taber (45)	--	--	50	--	80	--	80
Raymond (100)	35	50	100	--	100	--	120
Rosemary (22)	30	--	50	--	75	--	75+
Calgary (150)	75	105	90	75	120	90	135
Coaldale (36)	25	--	70	25	80	25	100
Lethbridge Honpa (225)	50	50	180	--	250	80	250

(N=15)

SOURCE: Organizational Questionnaire, 1983.
NOTE: *Statistics for Vancouver regular service is for their combined monthly family services.
--Dash means no data available.

Canada, the traditional O-Bon dance follows the
religious service.

Apart from these special occasions, the memorial
service (hoji) is the central ritual of the Buddhist
churches and performed at least once a month. Depending
on the dedication of the Buddhist member, a death in the
family can begin a long chain of other services. After
the funeral service, a memorial service is held on the
seventh day after a person's death, the forty-ninth day,
the one-hundredth day, and subsequently, on the first-
year anniversary, third-year anniversary, seventh-year
anniversary, and so on (Tsunoda, 1955:284-89).   In
Japanese society, the elaboration of these death-
oriented rites is what bound Buddhism to the Japanese
family with its traditional concern for ancestors.[9]
While these rituals were well-suited to traditional
Japanese society, they are an anomaly in contemporary
Canadian society.[10] The negative consequences of this
association between Buddhism and death are recognized by
BCC leaders.   The following excerpt from the 1983
"Message from the Chairman" (BCC) clearly expresses this
wide-spread concern:

> The concept of Buddhism and the Buddhist
> Church must be changed. Too often Bukkyo is
> related to death. How many times has one heard
> it said that it's too early to become a member
> of the Buddhist Church, "I wish I could do a
> little living before I join." Or a young
> chap would come to church and say, "This is
> where I come after death." The only time many
> of the young people come are to funerals and
> to memorial services. They come as a family
> unit. We must do our utmost to retain the
> attendance of the family--be it to volleyball,

> cooking demonstrations, flower arrangements,
> fun night where gaji, mah jong, bridge, etc.,
> can be played; as well as a place to recite
> the Nembutsu. The church should be a sociable
> and enjoyable place to come.

While death-oriented rituals appear to have little meaning for third-generation Japanese Canadians (Shimpo, 1981:20), they are regarded as the chief raison d'etre for Buddhist churches by the first generation. Until the first generation members (and possibly the second) disappear from the scene, these rituals will probably remain the central focus of the BCC.

In addition to these adult religious activities, Sunday schools have also been an important part of Buddhist church life in Canada. Since Buddhist priests had little or no experience with religious education for youth in Japan, their earliest Sunday schools were modeled after those found in the Christian churches. One of the most direct examples of borrowing from Christian sources can be seen in some of the early Buddhist Sunday school choruses. The lyrics of the traditional Christian tune, "Jesus loves me this I know, for the Bible tells me so," was modified to, "Buddha loves me this I know, for the Sutras tell me so" (Adachi, 1976:114). While Buddhists have made considerable efforts toward developing their own Sunday school curriculum, it is well-recognized that they have borrowed from Christian sources for many of their "ideas on the leadership and operation of a Sunday school" (Horinouchi, 1973:293).[11]

At the present time, most Buddhist Sunday schools are going through a period of decline. This is due in part to the natural generational changes which are

occurring. Many of the third generation are no longer
of Sunday school age and there are not yet many fourth
generation youth available for recruitment. Table III-4
presents data on the Sunday school programs currently
operated by the BCC (with the exception of the Vancouver
Buddhist Church). If the number of teachers and
students are combined, there are slightly over three
hundred individuals involved in the youth education
programs in Canada.

Social Organization and Foreign-Oriented
Character of the BCC

The foreign-oriented character of the BCC is
related not only to its organizational dependence upon
the Mother Temple in Kyoto, Japan, but also to the
"definitions of the situation" within the Japanese
Canadian community. For most Japanese immigrants in
Canada the Buddhist churches symbolized Japanese culture
and ties to the old country, whereas, Christianity was
viewed as the religion of Canada. Consequently, those
who affiliated with the Buddhist churches tended to be
more conservative and supporters of Japanese traditions,
while association with Christian churches was generally
regarded as a movement toward assimilation (Shimpo,
1977:123).[12]

Over the years, the strong orientation towards
Japanese culture has been gradually diminishing as the
number and influence of the immigrant generation in the
Buddhist churches has declined. Since they were born
and raised in Canada, the second and third generation
Japanese do not have such strong emotional attachments
to Japan. Although the psychological ties with Japan
may be on the wane, the following analysis of the

Table III-4

BCC Sunday School Programs, 1983

CHURCH	TEACHERS	SANSEI	YONSEI	CHILDREN OF NEW IMMIGRANTS	OTHER
Toronto	10	20	10	4	0
Montreal	1	4	0	0	0
Manitoba	3	15	0	3	0
Fraser Valley	2	7	0	5	0
Kamloops	6	10	0	0	0
Kelowna	10	10	15	4	0
Steveston	7	22	4	3	0
Raymond	10	20	7	8	1
Calgary	4	0	30	2	3
Coaldale	2	7	0	5	0
Lethbridge Honpa	3	25	0	0	0
Lethbridge Assoc.	--	5	0	0	0
TOTALS	58	145	66	34	4

SOURCE: Organizational Questionnaires and Interviews.
NOTE: --Dash means data not available.

organizational structure of the BCC and its dependence
upon Nishi Honganji clearly reveals the continuing
foreign-oriented character of this religious body. The
religious authority and legitimacy of the BCC is based
upon its relationship to the Lord Abbot (Monshu) of
Nishi Honganji. The Lord Abbot holds the highest office
in the True Pure Land School and is a direct descendent
of Shinran Shonin (1173-1262), the founder of Jodo
Shinshu. The Bishop of the BCC is regarded as the sole
representative of the Abbot for all religious matters in
Canada. Although nominated by the Ministerial Association of the BCC for this position, the Bishop's
authority is conferred upon him by the Abbot. Actual
appointment as Bishop requires a return to Nishi
Honganji, Kyoto, for an induction service.

While religious legitimacy is based upon the relationship to the Lord Abbot, the actual administrative
relationship and supervision of the BCC is conducted
through the International Department (Kokusaibu) of
Nishi Honganji. The International Department usually
sends a representative annually to visit the Buddhist
churches across North America. There are several
organizational levels within the BCC: the National,
District (Kyoku), and Congregational; each of these will
be considered in turn.[13]

At the national level, the BCC is managed by a
Board of twelve directors. Board members are nominated
and elected at the annual general meeting by delegates
from each of the churches and serve two-year terms of
office. The National Board has several functions. It
is the mediating administrative body between the
individual churches across Canada and the headquarters
in Japan. When additional ministers are needed and

finances are available, the National Board is responsible for making the request to the International
Department in Kyoto. This Board also manages various
accounts, such as the Minister's Training Assistance
Fund, the Minister's English Training Fund, and the
account for Religious Education. It also administers
grants sent from the International Department for
expenses related to the orientation and language
training of new priests from Japan. Due to the shortage
of priests in Canada, this Board in cooperation with the
Ministerial Association sponsors seminars for the
training of lay teachers.

The revenue required for the operation of this
Board comes from annual assessments made of all the
congregations within the BCC. Individual churches must
adopt the by-laws of the BCC and pay the annual dues for
membership and representation at the general meeting.
The funds collected from the member churches are used to
cover the expenses of the regular Board meetings, the
moving expenses of ministers across Canada, and pay the
annual dues to the International Department in Kyoto.
In addition to these annual dues, the BCC Board also
collects funds from all of the churches to send to Nishi
Honganji on special occasions. In 1977, for example,
the BCC sent approximately $3,000 to Nishi Honganji to
participate in the Inauguration Ceremony of the new Lord
Abbot. Over the next four years it was assessed by the
International Department and made payment of another
$22,000 as their contribution to the cost of a new
complex built to commemorate the appointment of the new
Abbot. The financial obligations to both the BCC
National Board and the Mother Temple in Kyoto has
resulted in considerable discontent among members of
many congregations. An active Nisei member of one

church explained this wide-spread dissatisfaction as
follows:

> The BCC is too costly. Since the churches are
> spread across Canada, it is expensive even to
> have a board meeting. Local congregations have
> a difficult time keeping themselves going, let
> alone paying for the BCC. People are not too
> happy about making financial donations to the
> Mother Temple either, since we get almost
> nothing back in return. But as local congrega-
> tions we are stuck because we have to get our
> ministers through the BCC and the Mother
> Temple.

Even though these financial responsibilities are
resented by some members, the fact that payments
continue to be made indicates that these churches
recognize their dependence upon the Mother Temple.
Since trained priests can only be recruited through the
International Department of Nishi Honganji, those
churches whose aim is to survive will undoubtedly remain
foreign-oriented for many years to come.

The Bishop of the BCC also serves as the Director
of the National Board. In that role he is expected to
attend all of the Board meetings, providing "religious
and administrative guidance and clarifying disputed
points of faith whenever necessary."[14] Along with the
general responsibility for the spiritual welfare of the
BCC, the Bishop has the more specific task of making all
ministerial appointments, transfers, and dismissals.
The Constitutional By-Laws of the BCC make it clear that
these duties are to be discharged in consultation with
the National Board, the Ministerial Association, and the
church members involved in the personnel changes. Due

to the current financial condition of the BCC, the
present Bishop is only employed on a part-time basis.
To supplement his income as Bishop, he also serves as a
part-time minister of the Toronto Buddhist Church.

The Ministerial Association consists of all the
Buddhist priests ordained by Nishi Honganji and employed
by one of the member churches of the BCC. Unlike in
Japan, where priests control both the religious and
financial affairs of the temple, priests in Canada are
regarded as "employees" hired by congregations to
provide religious services. The Association meets
annually and its members attend the general meeting of
the BCC. The number of votes controlled by priests at
this general meeting is suggestive of the minimal role
played by the Association in shaping the policies of
this organization. The total of 22 votes is distributed
as follows:

   1 - Bishop
   1 - Ministerial Association
   1 - National Board of Directors
   1 - Women's Buddhist Federation
  18 - Lay delegates from individual congregations

With lay delegates controlling most of the votes, it is
apparent that the priests are without significant
political power in this administrative structure.
Consequently, the Ministerial Association functions
primarily as a support group for priests facing similar
frustrations and difficulties.

As noted earlier, the Buddhist churches in Canada
are divided into the following four districts (Kyoku):
the British Columbia Buddhist Federation, the Alberta
Buddhist Federation, the Manitoba Buddhist Association,

and the Eastern District (Ontario and Quebec). Since
the BCC churches are scattered across Canada, the
district organization provides a mechanism for churches
within a particular geographical area to promote common
interests. The various districts usually hold at least
one conference a year giving area churches an opportunity to discuss mutual problems and concerns. In some
cases, the district organization is responsible for
arranging the service schedule of those ministers
serving several different churches (Kawamura, 1978:46).
The districts also sponsor fund-raising and social
activities. The six churches in the British Columbia
Federation, for example, support a Ministerial Training
Fund, the Young Adult Buddhist Association, and organize
sight-seeing parties to Japan.

At the congregational level, each church is managed
by a Board of Directors elected at an annual meeting.
In addition to this Board, the BCC churches consist of
several other sub-groups distinguishable by generation
and sex. The generational differences of language and
culture lead naturally to these separate associations.
The Toronto Buddhist Church, for example, contains the
following sub-groups:

Sangha: an English-speaking men's club for
Nisei with about 200 members;

Dana: an English-speaking club for Nisei
women with about 200 members;

Gohokai: a Japanese-speaking club for Issei
men with about 140 members;

Fujinkai: a Japanese-speaking club for Issei
women with about 200 members;

> Young Buddhist Association: an English-
> speaking club for Sansei youth.

These different associations within the Buddhist
churches sponsor a variety of social activities. Table
III-5 shows those social activities that are prominant
features of the BCC churches. The annual bazaar is the
most important fund-raising activity held in all of
these churches. As in many Protestant churches, these
associations also sponsor sports activities, annual
picnics, dances, and church dinners. The ethnic
character of the BCC churches is evident in the range of
activities related to their Japanese heritage including
Japanese cooking classes, flower arranging, Japanese
movies, and trips to Japan.

Conclusion

It is evident from the preceding discussion that
the BCC is still a foreign-oriented religious body
without organizational independence. Its religious
authority and legitimacy is still determined by the Lord
Abbot of Nishi Honganji. It also depends upon the
International Department in Kyoto for all of its
ministers. The BCC and Nishi Honganji are also linked
financially; the BCC sends annual assessment payments
and occasional special offerings to the Mother Temple,
and the International Department sends grants to the BCC
for the training expenses of new priests. Although Pure
Land Buddhism has been "Protestantized" (Horinouchi,
1973:3) to some degree in Canada, many of the rituals
and social activities of the BCC are still closely tied
to Japanese traditions and culture. In spite of the
considerable tension existing between the lay-oriented
congregationalism of the BCC and the hierarchical

Table III-5

Social Activities Organized and Sponsored
by the Buddhist Churches in Canada

CHURCH	DANCES/ SOCIALS	TRIPS TO JAPAN	JAPANESE COOKING	SPORTS	ANNUAL PICNIC	ANNUAL BAZAAR	JAPANESE MOVIES	OTHER
Calgary	x			x	x	x		
Coaldale					x	x		
Fraser Valley	x				x	x	x	
Hamilton						x		x
Kamloops	x		x		x	x	x	
Kelowna	x				x	x		x
Lethbridge*	x	x			x	x	x	
Lethbridge**	x				x	x	x	x
Manitoba	x				x	x	x	x
Montreal	x		x		x	x	x	x
Raymond	x		x		x	x	x	x
Steveston	x	x	x	x	x	x	x	x
Taber	x						x	
Toronto	x	x	x	x	x	x	x	x
Vancouver	x	x	x	x	x	x	x	x

N = 15
SOURCE: Organizational Questionnaire, 1983.
Note: *Lethbridge Buddhist Association; **Lethbridge Honpa.

priestly-oriented Mother Temple, the survival of the BCC for the foreseeable future will require cooperation with this administrative reference group overseas. The significance of this foreign-oriented character for organizational change and adaptation will be explored in more detail in subsequent chapters.

REFERENCES

1.   Tsunemitsu (1964:311) cites different dates than those reported by Ikuta for the time of this meeting and when Nishi Honganji actually approved the request for status as a separate missionary district. Tsunemitsu indicates that this meeting occurred in 1930 and approval by the Mother Temple was not granted until 1933. I have followed the account provided by Ikuta and mentioned in the brief history sketched in the Vancouver Buddhist Church 75th Anniversary Publication (1979:2-3).

2.   The Japanese Contribution to Canada, Canadian Japanese Association, Vancouver (1940:29), University of British Columbia, Special Collection, Japanese Collection. This report of Buddhist membership seems a bit exaggerated, but I have no other source to determine its degree of accuracy.

3.   Rev. Kawamura, one of the two priests permitted to remain in Canada, provided this information (Interview, 8 June 1983).

4.   These details were also provided by Rev. Kawamura (Interview, 8 June 1983).

5.   According to one informant, the Kyoku dissolved because of financial difficulties. Two years earlier the Kyoku had declined to hire a Nisei minister who had completed his Buddhist studies in Japan and was interested in serving the churches in Southern Alberta. The Raymond Buddhist Church then independently hired this Nisei as their resident priest and subsequently requested that their share of financing for the Kyoku minister (that is, the minister shared by all of the churches) be reduced. They could not afford to support both a Kyoku minister and a resident minister. With-drawal of financial support from the Kyoku by the Raymond Buddhist Church appears to be related to the disagreements and conflicts that ended in the schism of 1965.

6.   Minutes of BCC National Board of Directors Meeting, Vancouver, 23 January 1982.

7.   This brief outline of Jodo Shinshu beliefs is based upon interviews with priests and lay people, various tracts and pamphlets published by the BCC, and

Tsunoda (1955). While an indepth ethnographic study of religious beliefs would constitute a worthwhile project, it was beyond the confines of this organizational study.

8.   Kashima (1977) has noted that some of these modifications occurred in Japan after Buddhist priests visited Europe and the United States in the late nineteenth century. Reischauer observed some of these changes in Japanese Buddhism as early as 1917: "New methods of propaganda are being adopted, taken over bodily from Christianity. Thus on all sides we see springing up Young Men's Associations, Buddhist Sunday schools, Women's Societies, Orphanages, Homes for ex-convicts, etc. Even street preaching and special evangelistic campaigns are getting quite common, and the content of some sermons and hymns is sometimes taken bodily from Christianity, only that the name of Buddha takes the place of Christ" (Studies in Japanese Buddhism, New York: AMS Press, 1970:154). For similar observations in a more recent study, see Shigeyoshi Murakami, Japanese Religion in the Modern Century (tran. H. Byron Earhart, Tokyo: University of Tokyo Press, 1980:55-58).

9.   For a discussion of the relationship of Buddhism to death-oriented rites in Japanese society, see Tamaru Noriyoshi, "Buddhism," in Ichiro Hori, ed., Japanese Religion (Tokyo: Kodansha International, 1972:51-52).

10.   See Shimpo's (1981) discussion of the "base-institution" supporting ancestor worship in Japan. Japanese in Canada are no longer dependent upon the household (Ie), the traditional socio-economic unit in Japanese society which provided the basis for survival. Since the base-institution for ancestor worship did not develop in Canada, death-oriented rites become increasingly incongruous to successive generations of Japanese Canadians (1981:20).

11.   As in most Protestant churches, the typical Buddhist Sunday school program begins with a general assembly led by the Superintendent. Following introductory remarks and announcements, an opening hymn (gatha) is sung and children carry their offering forward to the altar. A lay leader or resident priest then leads the teachers and students in a traditional Japanese chant and in the recitation of the eightfold path. After a brief children's sermon, the students are dismissed to separate classes where traditional Japanese

stories, Buddhist beliefs and moral teachings, and arts and crafts form the basis of instruction.

12.   Before   the   Second   World   War,   the   foreign-orientation of Buddhists was not only related to their dependence upon the Mother Temple in Kyoto, but also to their stronger identification with Japanese Nationalism (Adachi, 1976:113).   Kawamura (1978:53) notes that before the war, Buddhist churches held special services for the Emperor's birthday.

13.   See Kashima (1977:172-180) for a discussion of the organizational structure of Jodo Shinshu in Japan and in the Buddhist Churches of America.

14.   By-Laws   of   the   Buddhist Churches   of   Canada, 1979:5.

CHAPTER FOUR: NATIVE-ORIENTED
MINORITY CHURCHES

Introduction

Native-oriented minority churches are those ethnic religious organizations operating in non-official languages that are sponsored by an indigenous Canadian church. Over the past century, various Christian denominations have engaged in missionary work among Japanese in Canada. Since Japanese immigrants regarded Christianity as the religion of Canada, affiliation with one of these missions symbolized movement into the host society.

It was not just the Japanese who viewed conversion to Christianity as a step in the assimilation process. This was also an assumption of many Christian leaders who shaped the vision guiding these evangelistic efforts. According to Clifford (1977:24), the arrival of many immigrants without a Christian heritage threatened the broad Protestant consensus in Canada; Christian denominations responded with a "crusade to Canadianize the immigrants by Christianizing them into conformity with the ideals and standards of Canadian white Anglo-Saxon Protestants." The United Church of Canada had the most successful denominational work among the Japanese. In addition to those Japanese integrated into Anglo-congregations, the United Church also contains the largest native-oriented minority church organization within the Japanese Canadian community.

Historical Development

The United Church work among Japanese in Canada was
built upon earlier efforts initiated by Japanese
Christians to evangelize their fellow-immigrants. In
1892, an evangelist from the Japanese Methodist Church
of San Francisco arrived in British Columbia and held
services in a number of Japanese communities.[1] Another
evangelist arrived the following year, sent by the
Japanese Christian Endeavor Society of Seattle, to work
among the Japanese in British Columbia. Ill health
forced him to leave his work after three years, but by
that time Christian missions had been established in
Victoria and Union. In 1896, a Japanese minister from
the Methodist Episcopal Church in Columbus, Ohio, came
to British Columbia to continue the work begun by these
lay evangelists. He consolidated these earlier efforts
and brought all the independent Japanese missions under
the supervision of the Methodist Church.

With the support of the Methodist Church, Japanese
missions continued to grow. The Missionary Society of
the denomination provided financial assistance so that
property and buildings could be purchased for the
Japanese work. The Women's Missionary Society helped
organize kindergartens and Sunday schools in many
missions. English night schools and orientation classes
for new immigrants were also an important part of the
Methodist work. By the 1920s, the Methodist work among
the Japanese in British Columbia consisted of six
missions, six missionaries, and an adult membership of
482.[2]

In 1925, the Methodists joined the Congregationa-
lists and Presbyterians to form the United Church of
Canada. The Methodist work among the Japanese continued

under the auspices of the United Church of Canada (Osterhout, 1929, 133-134). The centre of the United Church work with the Japanese remained in Vancouver. Between 1926 and 1942, almost 500 baptisms were performed in the Powell Street church alone. It was also in this church that Rev. K. Shimizu began special English services for the acculturated second generation and eventually organized a separate Nisei congregation in 1936.[3]

The United Church influenced many Japanese by providing English night schools, regular religious services, kindergartens, through-the-week clubs for children, Sunday schools, and women's association meetings. According to a 1935 survey, 4,789 of the 22,205 Japanese in British Columbia identified themselves with the United Church.[4] Not all of those identifying with the United Church, however, were in fact members. Table IV-1 shows that by the end of 1940 the United Church work among Japanese consisted of 8 churches with a membership of 1,070, and 21 Sunday schools with an enrollment of 1,294. In addition, there were also a number of kindergartens, women's groups, and children's clubs organized by the Women's Missionary Society (WMS) workers in Steveston, Victoria, Duncan, Chemainus, Vancouver, New Westminster, and Mission City.[5]

The government policy toward the Japanese during the Second World War forced the United Church Board of Home Missions to review its work among the Japanese. In a 1941 Memorandum to the British Columbia Security Commission, the Board expressed their concern for the welfare of the Japanese as follows:

We have it as our duty in these days of
terrible upheaval for our Japanese congregations, to follow them with our ministry and to
assure them of our sympathy. We also desire
by rendering this service to assure them that
a great Canadian Church, while realizing that
our Government must protect us so far as
possible from insidious attacks, wishes to
dissociate itself from vicious and unchristian
attitudes, and to hold fast the faith that in
Christ there is no distinction of race or
colour. Looking to the future, the United
Church wishes to continue its ministry to the
Japanese people, so that, whatever their final
disposition may be, it can serve them in the
future as it has in the past.[6]

Table IV-1

Japanese United Church Work in
British Columbia, 1940

LOCATION	CHURCH MEMBERSHIP	SUNDAY SCHOOLS	SUN. SCHOOL MEMBERSHIP
Cumberland	84	3	152
Fraser Valley	166	2	105
Kelowna	96	5	97
New Westminster	110	2	61
Ocean Falls	38	2	120
Steveston	156	1	129
Vancouver	326	3	473
Victoria	94	3	157
TOTAL	1,070	21	1,294

SOURCE: Memorandum Re Japanese Situation, 1941,
Vancouver School of Theology Archives, Vancouver, B.C.

Many Japanese were disappointed by the failure of the United Church to speak out against the radical measures taken by the government. Could the Christian Church support the mass evacuation and relocation of innocent Japanese children and adults?[7] What redeemed the United Church in the eyes of some Japanese was the fact that WMS workers and missionaries who had returned from Japan were all reassigned to work with the Japanese in the relocation centres. Throughout the war they worked with the Japanese ministers among the evacuated population in Kelowna, New Denver, Roseberry, Lemon Creek, Tashme, Kaslo, and Greenwood, British Columbia, and further east in Southern Alberta and Manitoba. In October 1943, Rev. W.R. McWilliams visited all of the Japanese settlements on behalf of the United Church Board of Home Missions. After seeing firsthand all of the hardships they faced and the losses they incurred, he poignantly remarked: "The evacuation business has uncovered the most unlovely page of our history, and whatever our people think of it, the day will come when we will be a lot less secure in it than we are at this hour."[8]

Japanese United Church ministers and WMS workers resumed their religious services among the evacuated Japanese as soon as they were reassigned. In the various camps in interior British Columbia, Sunday schools were established and both English and Japanese worship services were begun. Reports of the work in Tashme, for example, where over 2,500 Japanese had been relocated, reveal that attendance at United Church programs went as high as 80 for the Japanese language service, 120 for the English service, and up to 230 in Sunday school. Almost one hundred Japanese, predominantly second generation, were brought into formal membership through baptism as a result of these

efforts during the war.[9] Other camps had similar
services organized by the United Church workers,
although attendance tended to be lower.

In addition to religious services, United Church
workers made considerable efforts in the area of
education. Local school boards refused to accept
responsibility for educating Japanese children who had
moved into their districts as a result of the
evacuation. Also, some Japanese young people were
evacuated to areas where a public school system did not
even exist. The British Columbia Security Commission
finally assumed responsibility for compulsory education,
that is, elementary school. Representatives of the
Commission visited the camps to recruit volunteer
teachers, and make-shift schools were set up. Most of
the teachers for the elementary school programs were
second-generation Japanese Canadians who were already
high school graduates. The government made no
arrangements for high school students to continue their
education. United Church workers were appointed to
teach high school in several camps, but in most cases
this primarily involved the supervision of
correspondence courses. Not only did the churches
assume responsibility for high school education, they
also organized a number of kindergartens. The efforts
of United Church workers to meet the educational needs
of the young people helped establish respect for the
Christian church among some Japanese who were
disillusioned by the churches' earlier silence.[10]

The United Church of Canada was also concerned for
the welfare of those Japanese, primarily Nisei, who had
already moved to eastern Canada for resettlement. In
cooperation with the British Columbia Security
Commission, the Home Mission Board of the United Church

sent Rev. Shimizu, a bilingual minister serving the evacuated Japanese in Kaslo, to review the resettlement process in the east. Upon his return to British Columbia, Rev. Shimizu reported to the Conference of Japanese Workers (September 30, 1943), that the Japanese Christians who moved east "were so adapted that they have no thought of ever returning to British Columbia."[11] Although the resettlement process did present some problems, such as scarcity of adequate housing, Shimizu was convinced that resettling in the east was the best option for the Japanese. He was so certain, in fact, that he brought back movies of Japanese who had found new lives in the east to show among the evacuated families in British Columbia. Many resented his efforts to encourage Japanese to move east and disparagingly referred to him as a "government dog."[12]

In the spring of 1944, Rev. Shimizu was reassigned by the Home Mission Board to work with the Japanese Canadians relocated in Ontario and Quebec. After several months in his new position he realized that the adaptation of Japanese to conditions in the east had not been as complete as he reported the previous year. Although most were engaged in gainful employment, Shimizu discovered that the majority of relocated Japanese were also "restless, bewildered, and unhappy."[13] In a report on "Resettlement of Japanese Canadians" (June 21, 1944), Rev. Shimizu attributed this wide-spread depression and discontent to a number of factors, summarized as follows:

(1) Family separations: many of those initially relocated in the east were young people separated from their families for the first time.

(2) Occupational maladjustment: most were employed in positions totally different from those for which they were trained and in which they had been engaged in British Columbia before the war.

(3) Housing problems: many Japanese seeking adequate housing found that they were turned away because of their race.

(4) Resentment towards the government: the treatment of Japanese Canadians so differently from German and Italian Canadians, i.e., their evacuation and loss of property at the hands of the Custodians, led to deep resentment since it demonstrated that the Canadian government was dealing with citizens on the basis of race rather than citizenship or merit.

(5) Uncertainty regarding the future: Japanese could not help but wonder what the next government action would be in its quest for a solution to the Japanese problem; adverse public opinion, such as newspaper articles arguing for total repatriation of Japanese, necessarily created some uneasiness even among those in eastern Canada.[14]

All of these factors understandably generated a sense of insecurity and uprootedness, a condition that would not be significantly altered until after the war.

The United Church work among the Japanese was changed again when the federal government made its decision to repatriate all Japanese to Japan or resettle them in eastern Canada. Ministers and WMS workers were to be reassigned as the church followed the Japanese to their new locations. The choice of repatriation or resettlement was a source of considerable tension, and divided many families and the Japanese community. As early as April 1945, R.C.M.P. detachments were visiting the Japanese centres with application forms for repatriation. A Japanese United Church minister reported that after almost 90 percent of the Japanese in Lemon Creek signed the repatriation papers, the minority who agreed to leave British Columbia were under great pressure:

> Here in Lemon Creek, the people who had decided to relocate in Eastern Canada were afraid to tell the other people of their decision, since the majority of the people here in Lemon Creek considered such a decision as being disloyal to Japan and loyal to Canada. As a result, these people were sneered at and ridiculed. However, there was no actual physical violence committed. Naturally the people who had decided to go East wanted to get out of the atmosphere which was in Lemon Creek as quickly as possible.[15]

As Japanese settled in eastern Canada in increasing numbers at the end of the war, the administrators of the United Church initially discouraged the organization of ethnic congregations. In their view, the formation of distinct Japanese churches would encourage the growth of ethnic ghettos. Duplicating the pre-war situation, this would provide a clear target for racial discrimination for those who argued that the Japanese were unassimilable. According to Mitsui (1964:261), the "Home Missions Associate Secretary in Toronto was always the

chief promoter of this ideal of Japanese dispersement
and integration."

     In spite of this official church policy, Japanese
congregations were again organized as soon as there were
sufficient numbers and leadership.   The goal of
integrating Japanese into existing Anglo churches was
clearly premature.   Many of the first-generation
Japanese did begin to gather regularly for services in
Anglo churches, but they requested that someone be sent
to provide supplementary services in their own language
since they could not understand the religious services
in English.   The need for separate Japanese language
services was the first factor forcing the Board of Home
Missions to reconsider its policy and support the
formation of Japanese congregations.   A second factor
was the failure of many second generation Japanese to
attend and join the Anglo churches in their communities.
A survey of church attendance among Japanese United
Church families in Toronto revealed that only about 5
percent of those fifteen years or older were regular
participants in Anglo churches.[16]   The only way to
recover these members who were drifting away, in the
view of one Japanese Christian leader (Shimizu, 1944),
was to have Japanese ministers begin special outreach
programs for them.   Although the Nisei had no language
barrier preventing full participation in the existing
United Church, their experiences of racial discrimination kept many from becoming fully comfortable in
congregations that were dominantly Caucasian.   A
Japanese United Church Deaconness explained why an
ethnic congregation was needed even for the Canadian-
born generation:

     The Nisei felt the need to be by themselves to
     worship freely.   When they went to their local

> congregation, they felt like outsiders and
> soon lost interest in going. . . . In other
> words, a Nisei congregation was a necessary
> stepping stone to assimilation into a local
> congregation.[17]

These existing language and psychological barriers then
led naturally to the organization of distinct Japanese
congregations as they settled in new communities.

The Issei provided the primary leadership in the
formation of ethnic churches during the post-war period.
They began by holding home meetings, conducting services
in YWCA facilities, and meeting in Anglo churches when
facilities were not being used. Several of the Issei
congregations had their beginnings in the All People's
Churches, urban mission churches for various Non-Anglo-
Saxon communities. The distinct ethnic language
services that began in All People's Churches were viewed
by the Home Mission Board as temporary accommodations to
the immigrant generation. Malcolm MacDonald, the
Associate Secretary of the Home Mission Board, described
the role of these multi-ethnic mission churches as
follows:

> . . . the "language" churches' function is to
> help Non-Anglo-Saxon people to become merged
> or assimilated into the community and church
> life of the district in which they live. The
> second and third generations speaking English
> readily are encouraged to join and share in
> the life of the regular churches in their own
> areas (1951:53-53).

While the goal of the Home Mission Board was to facilitate assimilation through the All People's Churches, the

Issei congregations within these mission churches laid
the foundation for separate Japanese churches that would
include the English-speaking second and third
generations.

In 1944, the Issei in Winnipeg organized the first
Japanese congregation since the evacuation experience.
The Knox United Church, an Anglo-congregation, provided
a basement room for the Japanese to hold their services.
In eastern Canada, Issei congregations were formally
organized within All People's Churches in Toronto,
Hamilton, and Montreal during 1946. Just over a decade
later, the last Issei congregation was organized in
Vancouver. Since the Japanese were not allowed to
return to the coastal areas of British Columbia until
1949, the United Church work among the Japanese there
did not resume until the early 1950s. Services were
held in the First United Church for several years, and a
congregation formally organized in 1957.[18]

Shortly after the Issei congregations were
established, Japanese ministers began bilingual monthly
family services in an effort to draw in the Nisei who
were not attending the Anglo churches. Out of these
early family services Nisei fellowship groups were
formed. According to my informants, many Nisei
gravitated towards these groups in search of suitable
marriage partners. Since there was strong social
pressure from Issei to marry within the ethnic group,
even Nisei attending local churches eventually found
themselves involved in social activities with their
ethnic peers centered around Japanese churches. As
Nisei families were established, the need for regular
English services and Sunday schools became apparent.
With the growth in both Issei and Nisei religious and
social activities, Japanese congregations found it

difficult to continue as units within All People's Churches, meeting at times convenient with the host groups. Together, the Issei and Nisei sought greater independence that required separate church facilities. Fund-raising campaigns, grants, and loans from the Board of Home Missions made it possible for most of the Japanese congregations to purchase their own buildings. Approximately fifteen years after the war, Japanese congregations had been reestablished across Canada in Vancouver, Surrey, Okanagan, Lethbridge, Winnipeg, Toronto, Hamilton, and Montreal. In all of these locations both Japanese and English services were conducted to meet the needs of each generation. By 1962 the total adult membership of these churches had reached 1,311 and 343 young people were enrolled in six different Sunday school programs.

An interesting exception to the pattern of Issei and Nisei congregational development just described occurred in Steveston, British Columbia.[19] Prior to the Second World War, the Steveston Japanese United Church was a well-established congregation with 163 adult members, a Sunday school enrollment of 101, and its own land and facilities. The evacuation, of course, meant that the Steveston Japanese United Church was closed along with the others within the protected area. After 1949, some of the former members began returning to the area. Within two years, the Board of Home Missions reassigned a WMS worker and a missionary from Japan to resume work among Japanese in Steveston, Vancouver, and the Fraser Valley. The WMS worker organized a kindergarten, an English language night school, and several different youth organizations during the first year back in Steveston. By 1952, Rev. McWilliams was also conducting weekly worship services in Japanese. These distinct Japanese activities did not lead to the

organization of an ethnic church in Steveston, as they
had elsewhere in Canada. According to one account, the
Nisei in Steveston ". . . did not favor a separate
Japanese United Church, and urged the Issei to join with
the established United Church congregation. The United
Church people also were anxious that the Christians
should be one."[20] The small struggling Anglo church and
the group of Japanese Christians gathered in Steveston
decided that they needed each other. Representatives of
the Home Missions Board, officials of the Steveston
United Church, and representatives from the Japanese
congregation began serious discussions regarding the
amalgamation of these two groups. On February 15, 1953,
these two groups were officially united. When the two
congregations merged, the Japanese contributed their old
church property that had been held by the Home Mission
Board throughout the war years. At the time of the
amalgamation, the total membership was 136, composed of
64 Japanese and 72 Caucasians.

After the amalgamation, regular Japanese language
services were continued until Rev. McWilliams retired in
1956. The local English minister then began house
meetings for the Japanese, and bilingual elders served
as interpreters for his sermons. Over the past twenty-
five years, this integrated congregation has been under
the guidance of several different ministers, including a
Korean, a retired Caucasian pastor, and two Canadian-
born Japanese ministers. Although Steveston is an
amalgamated congregation, it is still recognized as a
part of the Japanese United Church Conference since the
members of the Japanese house meeting have continued to
pay the annual Conference fees. The Japanese membership
within this congregation has declined significantly
since this merger occurred. As of 1982, only 30
Japanese were counted among a total membership of 116.

Over the past two decades, some of the other Japanese congregations have also experienced a decline in membership. Collectively, nonetheless, the JUCC has experienced some growth during this same period. As indicated in Table IV-2, the JUCC currently has an adult membership of over 1,500 in its 11 congregations across Canada (this includes the Japanese membership of Steveston United Church). In Toronto and Vancouver, the two cities in Canada with the largest concentration of Japanese, the JUCC maintains separate congregations for the Japanese-speaking Issei and the English-speaking Nisei and Sansei. Each congregation has different ministers and separate church boards. In the other JUCC congregations, Issei and Nisei serve on the same board but have separate language services conducted.

Table IV-2
Japanese United Church Membership, 1983

CHURCH	MEMBERSHIP
Vancouver Issei	130
Vancouver Nisei	45
Fraser Valley	58
Steveston	30
Okanagan	78
Southern Alberta	65
Manitoba	110
Toronto Issei	316
Toronto Nisei	349
Hamilton	209
Montreal	122
TOTAL	1,512

SOURCE: Organizational Questionnaires and Correspondence.

Religious Beliefs and Activities

As pastoral charges of the United Church of Canada, the congregations within the Japanese Conference follow the pattern of doctrine and ritual set forth by the national church. Full membership in Japanese congregations requires acceptance of the confession of faith and baptism. Although the services established by the United Church are essentially maintained, the interpretation of Christianity has been altered by the background and experience of the Japanese. Japanese Christians have reshaped this tradition so that their ethnic heritage is still valued and integrated into the activities of the church. This point deserves further consideration and illustration.

In sermons, Japanese ministers interpret the relationship between Christianity and Japanese religions in a manner which provides a sense of continuity with and appreciation for the past. Japanese religious traditions are not regarded as pagan and something to be despised; rather, Japanese ministers expand upon the fulfillment motif of the New Testament and teach that both Buddhism and Shintoism have been made complete through the revelation of Jesus Christ. The tragic history of the Japanese evacuation, internment, and dispersal across Canada is also given religious significance through references to Biblical narratives. The success and upward mobility of the Japanese since the war is compared to the story of Joseph who, with God's help, turned misfortune into opportunity after being taken as a slave into Egypt (Genesis 37-45).

It is also apparent that the conception of Christianity among Japanese United Church members has been shaped largely by their ethnic heritage. Earhart

(1974:2-3) has observed that "Japanese traditions tend to
be mutually syncretistic, rather than mutually
exclusive." Since religions in Japan have rarely
"claimed absolute truth to the exclusion of all other
traditions," Japanese usually participate in various
religious traditions at different stages of the life-
cycle. This kind of orientation and understanding of
religious truth has been carried over in some measure
into the Japanese United Churches. One Nisei interviewed
explained that he accepted his father's understanding of
religion, summing it up as follows:

> There is only one Kami, there is only one God.
> When you draw a circle with a compass the
> centre of it is Kami. Where you stand around
> the circle are the different religions--
> Buddhism, Shinto, United Church, Roman
> Catholic--all looking to the centre.[21]

While noting this general orientation towards religion,
it is hardly surprising, one minister explained, that
Japanese have "come into the church for reasons other
than that they were convinced Christianity was true."

According to my informants, affiliation with the
United Church has usually not been due to a profound
conversion experience. Most explain that United Church
missionaries were helpful to the Japanese during their
difficult times of adjustment before the war, throughout
the evacuation experience, and during the period of
resettlement across Canada. Since Christianity is the
religion of Canada and the United Church is one of the
influential churches, joining was only natural for those
expecting to remain in Canada. A minister from Japan
for whom commitment to Christianity meant serious
religious reflection and decision found this attitude

toward faith and membership disheartening, as the
following incident reveals:

> The first time I was disappointed was when I
> took an elder out for personal evangelism and
> outreach with non-Christians. The Issei elder
> said to the people: "Christianity is the
> religion of Canada; it's your profit to become
> a Christian." For one who has come from
> Japan, that was a discouraging comment. Maybe
> he thought this was the best approach, but I
> was frustrated and tried to change that kind
> of attitude.

Undoubtedly, there are some individuals within the JUCC
whose membership is based upon a profound religious
experience and commitment. For the most part, however,
it seems that affiliation with the United Church has
been regarded as a part of the process of becoming
Canadian.

The ethnic heritage of Japanese Christians has not
only influenced religious consciousness, but also led to
modifications in religious ritual. In addition to
participation in the regular services and rituals
recognized by the United Church of Canada--baptism,
confirmation, communion--the Japanese Christians have
appropriated and modified the Buddhist memorial service
(see Table IV-3).[22] Although the memorial service is
not held monthly as in the Buddhist churches, there is
usually at least one memorial service held each year (in
some churches on Easter Sunday). At this service, the
names of the deceased from the various churches'
families are all read aloud. Numerous families also
have ministers conduct private memorial services at the
first year anniversary of the deceased. This carry-over

Table IV-3

Membership and Attendance in Japanese United Churches

CHURCH	MEMBERSHIP	REGULAR ATTENDANCE	EASTER	CHRISTMAS	MEMORIAL SERVICE
Hamilton	209	45	130	100	130
Fraser Valley	58	25	40	60	80
Manitoba	110	35	80	100	80
Southern Alberta	65	36	70	29	--
Montreal	122	35	70	80	50
Toronto Issei	316	--	600	600	500
Toronto Nisei	349	125	600	600	500
Vancouver Issei	130	55	30	40	30
Vancouver Nisei	45	35	30	40	30
Okanagan	78	56	91	91	91

SOURCE: Organizational Questionnaires.

NOTE: Statistics on attendance for Toronto and Vancouver are for joint Issei/ Nisei services at Easter, Christmas, and Memorial Services. Statistics for Okanagan include attendance at services held in three different locations.

from Buddhism also appears on other occasions. At the
1982 National Ethnic Convention, for example, the
Japanese Conference began with a memorial service for
all those members who had passed away during the
preceding two years. Thus, the traditional Japanese
concern for ancestors has been effectively transmitted
by Issei to their children, and has led to the
development of a ritual not commonly found in Anglo
United Church congregations.[23]

As the earlier historical sketch indicated,
religious education for youth has been a major concern
of United Church workers among the Japanese. Along with
kindergartens and Sunday school programs, Japanese
congregations have organized the full range of United
Church activities at various points during their
history. Following the natural generational life-cycles,
most Japanese congregations report a decline in the size
of their Sunday school programs over the past five
years. In spite of decline, Table IV-4 shows that over
four hundred individuals (students and teachers
combined) are still involved in the JUCC Sunday school
programs.

The social activities in Japanese United Church
congregations are similar to those found in the Buddhist
Churches of Canada (Table IV-5). The annual bazaar is
an important social event for all the churches and
usually attracts wide support from the larger Japanese
and Caucasian community. In most churches it remains
the key fund-raising method. The ethnic heritage of the
Japanese is clearly visible on this occasion, and
traditional foods such as sushi and udon are prepared
for sale. Another well-attended church-wide event is
the annual picnic.

Table IV-4
Japanese United Church Sunday Schools

CHURCH	TEACHERS AND STUDENT ENROLLMENT
Montreal	36
Toronto Issei	20
Toronto Nisei	158
Hamilton	85
Manitoba	39
Southern Alberta	19
Fraser Valley	12
Vancouver Issei	21
Vancouver Nisei	61
Steveston	12
TOTAL	463

SOURCE: United Church of Canada Year Book, 1982.
NOTE: Steveston is an amalgamated congregation with a
total of 49 involved in the Sunday School, 12 of whom
are Japanese.

Adults are also members of distinct groups within
the congregations. United Church Women's groups (UCW)
are active in most congregations. They engage in a
number of fund-raising activities for the larger mission
of the United Church as well as for financial needs of
the local church. On many occasions these women's
groups have promoted Japanese culture in other churches
by providing demonstrations in Japanese cooking, flower
arrangement, tea ceremony, and speaking about Japan.
Japanese congregations also contain other groups aimed
more at fellowship, entertainment, and recreation. The
Toronto church, for example, has a Nisei fellowship
group that has sponsored an annual dinner dance for
years with as many as four hundred attending. The

Table IV-5

Social Activities in Japanese United Churches

CHURCH	ANNUAL BAZAAR	ANNUAL PICNIC	JAPANESE COOKING	JAPANESE MOVIES	DANCES/ SOCIALS	SPORTS
Steveston	x	x				
Fraser Valley	x	x	x	x		x
Vancouver Issei	x	x	x			
Vancouver Nisei	x	x				
Montreal	x	x	x	x	x	x
Hamilton	x	x	x	x	x	x
Toronto Nisei	x	x	x		x	x
Manitoba	x	x	x	x	x	x
Southern Alberta	x	x	x			
Okanagan	x	x				

SOURCE: Organizational Questionnaire, Interviews, and Church Reports.

Hamilton church has a men's group that frequently sponsors sports films at the church and holds an annual golf tournament and fish fry. These few examples illustrate the diverse activities which make up the social life of Japanese congregations.

Besides the Sunday school programs, Sansei youth are involved in a number of other clubs and activities within these churches. Some Japanese congregations maintain the traditional United Church youth clubs, such as C.G.I.T (Canadian Girls in Training) for girls ages 12-14, and Explorers, a group for girls ages 9-11. These clubs meet for cooking and craft periods, hold Mother and Daughter Banquets, sponsor various parties, and assist with regular fund-raising activities of the church. Older Sansei in many churches also have groups that meet together for sports, movies, and retreats. All in all, the activities of Sansei youth in Japanese congregations differ little from the youth activities of the typical Anglo United Church.

Social Organization and Native-Oriented Character

The native-oriented character of the JUCC is based upon its relationship with the United Church of Canada and the "definitions of the situation" within the Japanese community. As noted earlier in this study, membership in one of the Christian churches was generally regarded by the Japanese as a movement toward assimilation and a part of the process of becoming a Canadian. This basic orientation and the supervision and support provided by the United Church make the JUCC a prime example of a native-oriented minority church organization.

For most of their history, the Japanese congregations of the United Church were under the direct supervision of the Board of Home Missions. The Board of Home Missions appointed superintendents to each of the United Church Conferences to oversee the ethnic missions, community missions, educational and medical work in each geographical area. The Japanese missions were primarily the concern of the superintendent of British Columbia until the end of the Second World War.

The role of this indigenous sponsoring body is evident in several areas. As far as the issue of religious leadership was concerned, it was the superintendent that made final personnel decisions: ministers were called from Japan and assigned to Japanese congregations by the superintendent. WMS workers were also assigned to various Japanese missions under the general direction of the Board of Home Missions. It should be recalled that the WMS workers were important agents of acculturation since they were largely responsible for the organizations of English classes, kindergartens, and Sunday schools in a number of Japanese communities. This native-orientation is also related to the financial dependence of the Japanese congregations upon the Board of Home Missions. Immigrants struggling to establish themselves in a new country often do not have the resources needed to purchase land and a building for a church, or to pay the regular salary of a minister. The United Church (and before it, the Methodist Church) through its Board of Home Missions provided grants and loans for land and buildings to be purchased for the Japanese missions. The income of Japanese ministers was subsidized by the Board, and the missions received the services of WMS workers without any financial obligation. During the war this relationship continued. The Home Mission Board

assigned personnel and provided financial support for
the continuation of mission work among the Japanese
relocated in interior British Columbia, Southern
Alberta, and Manitoba.

Since the war, the Board of Home Missions continued
to serve as the administrative reference group for many
Japanese members of the United Church. As noted above,
the Board initially encouraged Japanese to join Anglo
churches as they complied with the government policy of
geographical dispersal and resettlement. When this
approach was not successful, the Board did change its
position and support the reorganization of separate
Japanese congregations. The underlying goal remained,
nevertheless, assimilationist in orientation. This aim
of United Church missions was aptly summed-up by one of
the WMS workers, as follows: "In all our work we must
ever bear in mind the goal towards which we are
striving--that is the gradual integration of our people
into the existing churches."[24]

Even with this assimilationist goal, the Board
generously funded the Japanese work and made it possible
for Japanese to establish their own churches after the
war. Grants and low interest loans enabled several
Japanese congregations to move out of the All People's
Churches they shared and purchase their own facilities.
The Board also provided annual grants to assist with the
regular operating expenses. In 1961, for example, seven
of the nine Japanese congregations were receiving
financial aid from the Board totaling over $16,000.[25]
Thus, throughout most of their history, the Japanese
churches have been subsidized by the Board of Home
Missions. The Board also provided kindergarten teachers
and assisted with ministerial housing from time to time.
Without this ongoing support, the Japanese churches

would have followed an entirely different course of
development.

Organizational Change

Organizational changes within the United Church of
Canada since the early 1970s have significantly altered
the circumstances of the Japanese congregations
scattered across Canada. The Japanese churches along
with the other ethnic ministries in the United Church
are no longer under direct supervision, nor do they
receive support from the Board of Home Missions. This
supervisory body has been eliminated and now the ethnic
churches must go through the same administrative
channels as the Anglo churches. The new position of
Japanese congregations within the structure of the
United Church requires further elaboration.

At the present time, there are 2,391 pastoral
charges divided among 92 Presbyteries and 12 Conferences
in the United Church. Within the new structure, all
special funding (Block Grants) is administered by the
Conferences according to the recommendations of the
Presbyteries. The 11 Japanese churches spread across
Canada must now compete with Anglo congregations within
their own Presbytery for recognition. In essence, these
organizational changes have meant that the national
leadership for ethnic missions has been weakened and
ethnic congregations must fend for themselves in an
Anglo-dominated church bureaucracy.[26]

This administrative change provides the context for
understanding the current role of the Japanese United
Church Conference. While Japanese ministers and lay
delegates have met periodically throughout the history

of Japanese mission work in Canada, the need for an ethnic association and regular meetings appears to have become more acute in recent years. The sense of abandonment and lack of recognition within this new structure has made the Conference a more important support group for Japanese clergy. Some ethnic ministers feel that they do not have the status of Anglo clergy and cannot be as effective in the new organizational set-up. One Japanese minister expressed his frustration as follows: "In my own Presbytery I feel like I'm at the bottom of the totem pole. I am not recognized as an important voice and have no power." The concern of ethnic leaders is that Presbyteries will not be as sympathetic to their unique problems nor as supportive of their specialized ministries as the Home Mission Board was for many years.

Because ethnic churches face unique problems not adequately addressed by the sponsoring religious body, the Japanese Conference has become an important association. The key role of the JUCC is to provide opportunities for clergy and lay leaders from Japanese churches to meet together to solve these mutual problems. Much like the Ministerial Association in the BCC, the Conference is a support group for leaders encountering the same difficulties of ethnic ministry. Each Japanese United Church that subscribes to the Constitution and By-Laws of the Conference and submits the annual membership fee is considered a full member with voting privileges. At the General Meeting held every two or three years, each church is represented by one minister and one lay delegate.

The primary issue addressed by this Conference over the years has been the problem of religious leadership. Because of their Japanese-speaking membership, these

churches cannot draw from the general pool of available
United Church ministers. With only a few bilingual
Nisei ministers available, the Conference has had to
recruit ministers from Japan to provide services for
many of the Japanese congregations. The United Church
Block Grants do not cover the additional expenses of
moving a minister from Japan, so the membership dues
collected by the Conference have been used to assist its
member churches with this extra financial burden. The
smaller churches in the Conference would not be able to
call a minister from Japan without the financial
assistance provided by the other Japanese congregations.
While the JUCC must take the financial responsibility
for bringing ministers from Japan, it should be noted
that the sponsoring religious body still maintains some
control over this minority church. All Japanese
ministers are required to meet the educational and
doctrinal standards of the United Church of Canada.
Occasionally, Japanese ministers are required to take
additional course work in a United Church theological
college before they are given full status as clergy.

Along with recruitment, the Conference has also
coordinated all of the ministerial changes or rotations
within the member churches. The general policy of the
JUCC has been to change ministerial assignments every
five years, a procedure some ministers jokingly refer to
as "musical chairs." According to my informants, a
major consequence of the Conference negotiating these
ministerial changes has been a gradual loss of congregational power and choice. When the time of rotation
approaches, ministers submit their first and second
choices for a new assignment to the Conference.
Delegates from each of the churches also submit their
first and second choices for their next minister. The
Conference then attempts to work out new assignments so

that each church will be satisfied and no minister will be without a church. This method of rotation has meant that ministers are over-protected. The Conference informs the congregations of whom they will be calling as their next minister, rather than the churches contacting directly the minister they wish to call. Ministers are assured of a future job and never have to suffer "loss of face" by not receiving a call from one of the Conference churches.

The fact that ministers tend to dominate the Conference activities, discussions, and decisions has led to apathy among some lay delegates. In their view, it is primarily for the benefit of the ministers that these Conference meetings are held. While recognizing that it is the Japanese clergy who have the primary motivation for keeping the JUCC in operation, it would be wrong to imply that the Conference is simply a self-serving organization for ministers. The Conference has also sponsored activities benefiting all the Japanese churches. Periodically, for example, the JUCC sponsors a speaker from Japan to visit all of the congregations across Canada. This is an event none of the churches could afford to undertake independently. Several years ago the Conference also intervened to help the Japanese church in Southern Alberta which was about to fold. A minister was sent to study the situation and recommended that the church remain open. The Conference then collectively requested additional financial aid from the Alberta Conference and reassigned a Nisei minister to the church in an attempt to revitalize the congregation. These few examples sufficiently illustrate the various functions performed by an ethnic conference within an indigenous religious body.

The foregoing analysis suggested that ethnic churches have had difficult adjustments to make with the removal of direct supervision and support by the Board of Home Missions. More recent ideological changes within the United Church, nevertheless, indicate a more positive attitude toward ethnic churches. In the current environment of Canadian multi-culturalism, the United Church has abandoned its earlier held goal of assimilation. At the 1982 National Ethnic Convention organized around the theme, "Unity Without Uniformity," a new "Ethnic Ministry Policy and Guidelines" paper from the Division of Mission in Canada was distributed. The new policy paper rejected the inherited assumptions that guided the ethnic ministries in the past: ethno-centrism, paternalism, and assimilationism. With different expressions of theology and ways of worship, the paper explains, ethnic peoples have a special contribution to make to the United Church of Canada. The paper also confesses that:

> In a day when the country is more and more
> multi-cultural, the United Church has
> decreased ethnic ministries. Although numbers
> of ethnic people are increasing in Canada, the
> United Church of Canada is providing less
> funding and fewer personnel than formerly so
> that the perception may be that the United
> Church is a WASP enclave.[27]

In the case of the Japanese Conference, this statement is not entirely accurate. While Japanese congregations no longer have WMS personnel working with them, the JUCC has managed to obtain grants for the smaller Japanese churches in spite of the new funding arrangement. In 1980, for example, 5 of the 11 Japanese churches were

still funded from Block Grants for a total of over
$23,000.[28]

Although the JUCC has not fared too badly, there is
a growing concern among United Church policy makers that
ethnic minorities do not have a significant voice within
the structure of the church to shape their own future.
Since the United Church has had no national policy on
ethnic ministries for the past decade, Presbyteries and
Conferences have not responded to ethnic congregations
in a uniform manner. Differential treatment across
Canada has generated discontent among various ethnic
groups. In order to alleviate this problem, the
Division of Mission established a National Ethnic
Committee. This new committee is composed of members
elected at the National Ethnic Convention by
representatives from all of the ethnic churches. The
purpose of this committee is to assist in the
development of United Church policy toward ethnic work
and by providing consultation to help eliminate some of
the disparity of responses to ethnic churches in various
Presbyteries and Conferences. It is not yet clear how
effective this committee will be nor what significance
this new United Church attitude toward ethnic ministries
will have upon the future of minority churches.

REFERENCES

1.   This historical sketch draws upon a number of
works, including: Kanada Nikkeijin Godo Kyokai Shi (A
History of the Japanese Congregations of the United
Church of Canada, 1892-1959), published by the National
Japanese United Church Conference in 1961; Tadashi
Mitsui, "The Ministry of the United Church of Canada
Amongst the Canadians of Japanese Origin, 1892-1949,"
Master of Sacred Theology thesis, Union College, 1964;
and Kenneth Matsugu, "A Brief History of the Japanese
United Church of Canada," in Sumio Koga, ed.
A Centennial Legacy: A History of Japanese Christian
Missions in North America, 1877-1977 (Chicago: Nobart,
1977).

2.   Reported in the 101st Annual Report of the
Missionary Society of the Methodist Church of Canada,
1924-1925, Victoria University, United Church Archives,
Toronto.

3.   Rev. Shimizu was well-prepared for his bilingual
ministry. He had attended high school in New
Westminister, was a graduate of the University of
British Columbia, and had received his Master's degree
from Harvard in 1924.

4.   The results of this survey are recorded in the
Report of the Life and Work Committee, British Columbia
Conference, United Church of Canada, 1935, United Church
Archives, Vancouver School of Theology.

5.   See the Memorandum Re Japanese Situation, British
Columbia Board of Home Missions, United Church of
Canada, 1941, United Church Archives, Vancouver School
of Theology.

6.   Memorandum Re Japanese Situation, 1941:4.

7.   Even the 18 Japanese children in the Women's
Missionary Society Oriental Home in Victoria, British
Columbia, were evacuated from the "protected area" to a
WMS school in Assiniboin, Saskatchewan (see Japanese
Canadians, 1942-1946, A Scrap Book, WMS Home Missions
Oriental Work; United Church Archives, Victoria
University, Toronto.

8.   Report of the Itinerary of Rev. W.R. McWilliams,
19 October 1943, p. 10; United Church Archives, Victoria
University, Toronto.

9.   Further details regarding the United Church work
among the Japanese in interior British Columbia,
Southern Alberta, and Manitoba during the war can be
found in Kanada Nikkeijin Godo Kyokai Shi (1961:93-120);
"History of Japanese Canadian United Church: English
Contributions," by various WMS missionaries, in the
Yasutaro Yamaga Papers, University of British Columbia,
Japanese Collection.

10.   These observations are based upon an interview
with Mrs. Hide Shimizu (12 June 1982, Toronto), formerly
Hide Hyodo, a Nisei who was recruited by the Secretary
of the British Columbia Security Commission to help set
up these educational programs during the war. Details
regarding the education of Japanese youth in these
centres during the war can also be found in the
Digest of the Minutes of the Conference of Japanese
Workers (1943), and in the Report of the Itinerary of
Rev. W.R. McWilliams (1943).

11.   Recorded in the Digest of the Minutes of the
Conference of Japanese Workers, 30 September 1943;
United Church Archives, Vancouver School of Theology.

12.   Mrs. Hide Shimizu, Interview, 12 June 1982,
Toronto, Ontario.

13.   Report Made by Rev. K. Shimizu on Resettlement of
Japanese Canadians, 21 June 1944; United Church
Archives, Victoria University, Toronto.

14.   Ibid.

15.   Rev. T. Komiyama, Report for the Month of April,
1945; United Church Archives, Vancouver School of
Theology.

16.   See Hide Shimizu, "A Brief History of the Nisei
Church," in Toronto Nikkeijin Godo Kyokai, 1946-1971,
Toronto,   1974:53.

17.   Grace Namba, Report of the Nisei Work in Eastern
Canada, n.d., p.3.

18.   For details regarding the developments of Japanese congregations during the post-war period, see Kanada Nikkei jin Godo Kyokai Shi (1961:118-52).

19.   Data for this discussion have been drawn from several interviews and the following historical materials: F.E.   Runnals,   A History of the Steveston United Church (1965), United Church Archives, Vancouver School of Theology; and Hedwig Bartling, "Steveston After World War II," in "History of Japanese United Church in Canada: English Contributions," Yamaga Yasutaro Papers, University of British Columbia, Japanese Canadian Collection.

20.   Hedwig Bartling, "Steveston After World War II," op. cit.

21.   The relationship between the Hamilton Buddhist Church and the Japanese United Church illustrates further the general lack of concern regarding ideological differences or competing truth claims. During the first few years of their existence there was a sense of competition and conflict because both congregations were actively seeking members and support for their activities from the Japanese community in Hamilton.   In recent years the sense of competition has diminished.   There seems to be a mutual concern to support any ethnic institution.   When the two churches celebrated their twenty fifth anniversaries   they sent small checks of congratulations to each other.   On another occasion, the Buddhist church sent one of its members as a representative to attend the dedication service for the new educational building at the Japanese United Church.   The Japanese United Church also loaned its movie projector to the Buddhist Church when their visiting Bishop wanted to show films of his recent pilgrimage in Asia.   These additional examples sufficiently show that ethnic ties transcend ideological differences and evangelical missionary zeal.

22.   See Reid (1981) for a helpful analysis of this type of cultural adaptation in Christian churches in Japan.

23. While this Japanese   background   has been influential, it should also be noted that the multi-cultural environment of Canada has also shaped the nature of activities in JUCC congregations.   A 35th Anniversary luncheon I attended in one Japanese United Church provides ample illustration.   The food for this

festive occasion was catered by a Chinese restaurant and
the Sansei and Yonsei (fourth generation) provided an
interesting program of entertainment, which included; a
violin solo, Japanese dances, a folk-rock group, and a
Yonsei (from a mixed marriage) performing two Highland
dance numbers. The ethnic diversity of the program led
the MC to jokingly remark that "the church did not
discriminate against other ethnic groups" (Author's
field notes, 4 October 1981).

24.   Miss Madeline Bock, "Okanagan Valley Japanese
Work," in "History of Japanese United Church in Canada:
English Contributions," Yamaga Yasutaro Papers,
University of British Columbia, Japanese Collection.

25.   This information was included in the Japanese
Congregations of the United Church of Canada Comparative
Report: 1959 and 1961. According to an Issei minister,
this special support made it possible for many Japanese
churches to avoid the high indebtedness of Anglo congregations engaged in similar building programs.

26.   Rev. Gordon Hume, a staff person at the Division
of Mission in Canada and Liaison Officer with the
National Ethnic Committee, emphasized this point in an
address to ethnic pastors and delegates at the National
Ethnic Convention (Author's field notes, 2 July 1982).

27.   Ethnic Ministry Policy and Guidelines Paper,
Division of Mission in Canada, United Church of Canada,
1982:2.

28.   Report of the 10th National Japanese United Church
Conference, Calgary, Alberta, May 4-6, 1981:8.

CHAPTER FIVE
GENERATIONAL CHANGE AND ORGANIZATIONAL
ADAPTATION: A COMPARATIVE ANALYSIS

Introduction

What significance do the divergent orientations of
the BCC and JUCC have upon generational change and
organizational adaptation? This broad question provides
the focus for the following discussion.

As indicated in Chapter One, minority churches can
be viewed from two different perspectives. According to
one point of view, minority churches "constitute a
strong force for ethnic persistence" and are an
indicator "of ways in which people are trying to
maintain their language and succeeding" (Millett,
1979:191-93). Are Japanese minority churches actually
effective as "base-institutions" (Shimpo, 1981:20) for
ethnic persistence? The following hypothesis derived
from the typology provides the framework for exploring
this question: since the BCC is foreign-oriented, it
has probably exerted greater effort towards maintaining
the Japanese language and culture than the native-
oriented JUCC. The analysis below will compare the
efforts and success of these two organizations in
maintaining their ethnic heritage.

From another perspective, minority churches can be
seen primarily as adapting organizations. This line of
thought assumes that the powerful forces of assimilation
will invariably transform an ethnic group over the
course of several generations and require internal
adaptations on the part of minority churches to survive.

Within an environment favoring Anglo-conformity,
minority churches must adapt in order to meet the needs
and attract the interest of increasingly acculturated
generations. Once the language shift occurs among the
second and third generations, organizational changes
become necessary in several areas. Bilingual religious
leaders must be recruited and additional English
language services and church schools must be
established. The materials used in religious services
and educational activities must also be made available
in both languages. Given the rapid assimilation of the
Japanese in Canada, it would be surprising if these
minority churches had not begun to make some
accommodations to the acculturated generations.

A hypothesis derived from the typology related to
this assimilationist perspective on organizational
development is that the native-oriented minority
churches are more likely to make the language adaptations than foreign-oriented churches. There are several
reasons one could expect native-oriented churches to be
better able to make these changes. First, native-
oriented churches are sponsored by an indigenous church
and would therefore be more naturally encouraged to
conform to the language and practices of the host
society. Foreign-oriented churches, on the other hand,
are organizationally linked to the old country
encouraging the preservation of ethnic language and
culture. The mother church which constitutes the
primary administrative reference group for these
churches, would tend to be more conservative and
resistant to adaptations that would diminish its power
and the dependence of the immigrant churches. Second,
the membership in native-oriented churches would tend to
be less conservative and more willing to adapt the

internal program and activities than the membership in foreign-oriented churches. The reasoning here is as follows: since members of native-oriented churches have identified with an indigenous church rather than maintaining ties with the religion of the old country, they are probably more assimilationist in orientation and willing to make organizational adaptations when necessary. Finally, as organizational adaptations are required of minority churches, native-oriented churches are more likely to be administratively prepared to make the necessary adjustments. Foreign-oriented churches with their dependence upon the parent organization overseas would tend to receive religious leaders ill-prepared for cross-cultural work. Trained in the language and customs of the old country, these pioneer missionaries would probably be neither inclined nor equipped to make the adaptations needed. Native-oriented churches have an indigenous sponsoring organization and educational institutions; they should therefore more easily recruit leaders who are able to effectively work with the acculturated generations. This assimilationist perspective will also be evaluated below.

Ethnic Persistence

Is there empirical evidence to support the view that Japanese minority churches are a strong force for the maintenance of ethnicity? Has the BCC been more concerned to preserve ethnicity than the JUCC, and has either minority church organization been successful? Ishwaran (1980:7) has suggested that "a group's commitment to ethnic identity and culture is directly proportionate to its capacity to preserve its linguistic identity." This discussion will begin by analyzing

language maintenance in these two organizations and
conclude with a consideration of endogamy, another key
indicator of ethnicity.

Language Maintenance

A comparison of the data in Tables V-1 and V-2
indicates that the foreign-oriented BCC has shown a
greater concern for maintaining the Japanese language.
During the post-war period, ten congregations within the
BCC have had Japanese language schools for a total of
159 years. By contrast, only three congregations within
the JUCC have had Japanese language schools for a total
of only 14 years.

Although the BCC has exerted greater efforts in
this area, neither organization has been successful in
generating or maintaining enthusiasm for the study of
Japanese among Sansei. Currently, both of these organizations are operating only one language school each with
a combined enrollment of 11. It is interesting to note
that the five students enrolled in the Manitoba Buddhist
Church language school were all Caucasian.

Tables V-1 and V-2 also show the responses of Nisei
church leaders to the question: "Approximately what
percentage of your Sansei can read and write Japanese?"
The estimates provided by Nisei respondents clearly
suggest that efforts to maintain the Japanese language
have largely failed within both minority church organizations. Respondents from the BCC churches on the
average estimate that less than 6 percent of their
Sansei can speak Japanese and less than 2 percent are
able to read and write Japanese. On the average, Nisei
respondents from the JUCC reported that approximately

Table V-1

Japanese Language Schools in the BCC and
Sansei Language Ability, 1983

CHURCH	NUMBER OF YEARS WITH SCHOOL	CURRENT ENROLLMENT	SANSEI JAPANESE ABILITY	
			SPEAKING	READING/WRITING
Steveston	20	0	10(%)	0(%)
Manitoba	30	5	0	0
Lethbridge Honpa	1	0	0	0
Lethbridge Assoc.	35	--	--	--
Kelowna	20	0	--	0
Montreal	4	0	--	--
Calgary	0	0	0	0
Toronto	--	0	--	--
Coaldale	0	0	--	--
Hamilton	0	0	1	0
Fraser Valley	2	0	20	10
Kamloops	25	0	10	5
Taber	2	0	0	0
Vancouver	0	0	15	5
Raymond	20	0	0	0
Rosemary	0	0	0	0

SOURCE: Organizational Questionnaire.

NOTE: --Dash means no data available.

Table V-2

Japanese Language Schools in the JUCC and

Sansei Language Ability, 1983

CHURCH	NUMBER OF YEARS WITH SCHOOL	CURRENT ENROLLMENT	SANSEI JAPANESE ABILITY	
			SPEAKING 0(%)	READING/WRITING 0(%)
Steveston	0	0	0	0
Manitoba	9	6	0	0
Montreal	3	0	50	10
Okanagan	0	0	0	0
Southern Alberta	--	0	0	0
Vancouver	0	0	10	10
Toronto	0	0	10	5
Fraser Valley	0	0	70	50
Hamilton	2	0	5	5

SOURCE: Organizational Questionnaire.

NOTE: --Dash means no data available.

10.5 percent of their Sansei are able to speak Japanese, and about 9 percent are able to read and write. While these are only crude measures of language ability, the estimates of almost all of these respondents (and confirmed by other informants interviewed across Canada) indicate that the maintenance of ethnic language among the third generation has been the exception rather than the rule.

Intermarriage

An examination of endogamy should provide further clarification of the role of minority churches in maintaining ethnicity. In Chapter Two it was noted that studies of Sansei marriages indicate a definite trend toward exogamy. Makabe's (1976:216) study of Canadian-born Japanese in Toronto revealed that 86 percent of the Sansei married outside the ethnic community. Similarly, Hirabayashi's (1978:63-65) study of Sansei intermarriage in Southern Alberta between 1970 and 1974 discovered exogamous rates of 82 percent in Lethbridge and 71.4 percent in Taber. Is this tendency toward exogamy among third-generation Japanese Canadians resisted in minority churches? Do these churches enforce a rule of endogamy, and is the foreign-oriented BCC more effective than the JUCC in discouraging intermarriage and maintaining the ethnic group?

Data presented in Tables V-3 and V-4 show the number and percentage of intermarriages among Sansei in the BCC and JUCC. Although data on this issue was not obtained from all of the Japanese churches, adequate data on churches across Canada indicates that a strong tendency towards exogamy exists even among Sansei affiliated with these institutions. The BCC (N=9)

reports that 163 Sansei marriages out of 217 are with
non-Japanese; that is, an intermarriage rate of 75.1
percent.[1] Five other BCC congregations estimated Sansei
intermarriage rates at between 70 and 100 percent but

Table V-3
Intermarriage Rates of Sansei in the BCC

CHURCH	NO. TOTAL MARRIAGES	NO. INTER- MARRIAGES	PERCENT INTERMARRIAGE
Raymond	47	39	82.9
Taber	20	10	50.0
Kelowna	16	8	50.0
Kamloops	50	40	80.0
Fraser Valley	12	7	58.3
Manitoba	24	18	75.0
Montreal	17	16	94.1
Hamilton	19	14	73.6
Coaldale	12	11	91.6

SOURCE: Organizational Questionnaire and Interviews.

Table V-4
Intermarriage Rates of Sansei in the JUCC

CHURCH	NO. TOTAL MARRIAGES	NO. INTER- MARRIAGES	PERCENT INTERMARRIAGE
Toronto	32	16	50.0
Hamilton	17	15	88.2
Vancouver	14	13	92.8
Fraser Valley	10	4	40.0
Manitoba	12	12	100.0
S. Alberta	12	9	75.0
Steveston	4	4	100.0

SOURCE: Organizational Questionnaires and Interviews.

provided no actual statistics. The JUCC (N=7) reports that 73 Sansei marriages out of a total of 101 are with non-Japanese; again, an intermarriage rate of over 70 percent.

The data examined on language maintenance and endogamy indicates that the cultural and marital assimilation of Sansei affiliated with minority churches corresponds closely to the findings of earlier studies. When placed in a historical perspective, the view that minority churches are a "strong force for ethnic persistence" is clearly untenable. Although minority churches tend to be conservative and make some efforts to preserve their ethnic heritage, the objective indicators of language and endogamy reveal a steady decline in ethnicity.

Organizational Adaptation

The other perspective on minority churches views them primarily as adapting organizations. Here it is assumed that assimilation is the dominant force shaping their development. The acculturation of native-born generations eventually forces minority churches to choose between accommodation and extinction (Niebuhr, 1957:203-12). This approach to minority churches recognizes that: "As the environments of organizations change, organizations must, if they are to persist, be able to adapt goals, structure, and services" (Zald and Denton, 1963:214). Meeting the needs and demands of the changing clientele, in the case of minority churches, means providing religious leadership and services in their first language. Successful recruitment of members from among the acculturated generations, therefore, requires increasing "Anglification" (Hofman, 1972:621).

The essence of this position has been captured by
Fishman (1972:50) when he states: "the more
'successful' religion becomes, the more **de-ethnicized**
it becomes, the more amenable to mergers with other de-
ethnicized churches, and the more disinterested in
language maintenance." (Emphasis mine.)

On the basis of the typology, it is hypothesized
that the native-oriented JUCC has been better able to
make the required adaptations than the foreign-oriented
BCC. In order to test this hypothesis, the following
analysis will focus upon religious leadership and
language adaptations in these two organizations. Before
examining data collected from churches across Canada,
the findings of the initial comparative case studies
will be briefly presented.[2]

Two Case Studies

The two churches under consideration were both
organized in Hamilton, Ontario, shortly after the Second
World War. Approximately 1,000 Japanese settled in
Hamilton following their evacuation, internment, and
geographical dispersal east of the Rockies. It was from
this pool of potential recruits that the Hamilton
Japanese United Church and the Hamilton Buddhist Church
drew their earliest members.

The Hamilton Japanese United Church: In spite of
the official United Church policy discouraging the
formation of Japanese congregations in eastern Canada,
many of the Christian Issei began to gather regularly at
two of the United Churches in downtown Hamilton. Since
they could not understand the religious services in
English, they requested that someone be sent to provide

additional services in Japanese. Responding to this request, a Japanese minister from Toronto began coming twice monthly to conduct these special services.

In 1946, the Issei formally organized their own congregation within one of the United Churches in downtown Hamilton. Due to a shortage of Japanese ministers, the congregation was led and supervised by women missionaries and part-time Japanese ministers for about nine years.[3] The group of 44 Issei finally obtained a resident Japanese minister in 1955. Even though as many as 70 Nisei attended the church-sponsored social activities for the Japanese young people, they had not been brought into the membership of the Japanese congregation.[4] The presence of a resident minister was quickly felt. Within five years the membership more than doubled, and an English-speaking congregation of 33 Nisei was organized.

With a rapidly growing membership, the Japanese congregation had visions of having its own separate church facilities. A grant of $5,000 and a loan of $13,000 from the United Church Board of Home Missions made it possible for them to purchase property and a building in 1962. The move into their own quarters was followed by an increase in social activities. After three years in their new location, the adult membership reached 151 (83 Issei, 68 Nisei) and 56 Sansei were enrolled in the Sunday school program.

Three other ministers have provided the leadership for this congregation since 1967. Each one has been bilingual and has continued services in Japanese for the Issei, and in English for the rest of the congregation. According to the 1981 Annual Report there were 206 confirmed members. Clearly noticeable are the generational changes affecting the composition of the congregation. The Issei membership has declined to 40, and only about one-fourth of them are able to attend services on a regular basis. At the present time, the 78 Nisei members provide the largest amount of financial support and lay leadership for the church. Over the past twenty years, the most significant growth has been among the third generation. There are 80 confirmed Sansei, and 33 others under fifteen years of age who are enrolled in the Sunday school. The remaining eight members are all post-war immigrants.

The Hamilton Buddhist Church: The Japanese Buddhists settling in Hamilton after the war did not have an existing church to accommodate their religious services. Nevertheless, within a short time they began meeting on a regular basis in the homes of the more dedicated Issei. Under the supervision of a Buddhist priest from Toronto, a congregation was formally organized in 1946. Two years later a house in the north end of the city was purchased and remodeled to serve as their church. It is estimated that between 60 and 80 members were involved in the church during the early years.[5] While the Issei dominated the church in both numbers and leadership, the Nisei also organized a small junior congregation.

Because of their small size and limited financial resources, the Hamilton Buddhist Church was unable to support a full-time minister for almost twenty years. All of the religous services were conducted by visiting priests and lay leaders until 1965. At that time, a Buddhist priest came from Japan and served as their first resident minister for three years.

Shortly after the minister's return to Japan, the church had another major adjustment to make. Due to a redevelopment project in the north end of the city, the church was forced to relocate. They purchased and moved into a building in the east end of the city, far removed from any of the residential areas of the Japanese population. This move was followed by a gradual decline in attendance and membership.

In an effort to involve Sansei in the church, the second-generation leaders organized an English Sunday school in the mid 1950s. Parental support for this program was so minimal that the teachers had to pick up the children themselves. While between 12 and 20 young people were involved in this program at one time, by 1970 there were more teachers than students and the Sunday school folded. The collapse of the Sunday school merely reflected the waning interest among the adults. By 1972, the membership declined to an all-time low of 45.

A small and dedicated group maintained the church over the next few difficult years. With some financial assistance from the BCC, the Hamilton congregation acquired its second resident minister in 1977. During his three years in residence, the number of religous services and social activities was increased and better attended. Since his retirement in 1980, the church has again been dependent upon visiting ministers and lay leaders. Consequently, services and activities are being reduced. Services were once conducted every Sunday; they are now held only once a month. According to the 1981 record, there is a total membership of 74 (42 Issei, 32 Nisei). There are no third-generation members at the present time.

The weakness of the Buddhist Church and the
relative strength of the Japanese United Church appears
to be closely related to several factors. The availability of religious leaders has certainly been a
decisive factor in the development of these two
congregations. The Japanese United Church obtained
their first resident minister in 1955 and have had a
minister since that time. The Buddhist Church, by
contrast, did not secure a resident minister until ten
years later. Furthermore, they have only had a resident
minister for six years of their thirty-five year
history. They lacked leadership at a crucial period
when the Japanese United Church had an energetic
minister who organized both an English-speaking
congregation and a Sunday school. Also, the ministers
of the Japanese United Church have all been bilingual,
whereas, the Buddhist priests only conducted services in
Japanese.[6] The failure to provide bilingual services
has doubtless been an inhibiting factor in the growth of
the Buddhist Church.[7] Finally, the two congregations
have had to deal with disparate financial situations.
The Board of Home Missions provided encouragement and
financial support for the Japanese United Church.
Grants and loans made it possible for them to purchase
facilities in a location ideal for the Japanese
population. The small Buddhist Church had minimal
outside support and found it necessary to purchase a
building in the east end of the city, an inconvenient
location where only the most dedicated have continued to
attend.

These two case studies support the basic hypothesis
regarding organizational adaptation derived from the
typology. With its dependence upon a Mother Temple
overseas, the Buddhist Church was unable to make the
necessary adaptations. The lack of bilingual priests

and English services are surely major factors accounting for the absence of third-generation involvement. By contrast, the relationship of the Japanese United Church to an indigenous sponsoring organization has facilitated adaptation and growth. Although these initial findings support the hypothesis, it is necessary to consider data on the other minority churches scattered across Canada in order to determine if these case studies are representative or typical. Since the ability of churches to make adaptations largely hinges upon their securing bilingual priests or ministers, the following discussion will begin with a comparative analysis of religious leadership in these two organizations.

Religious Leadership and Language Adaptations

Because of the Japanese Canadian experience of evacuation and resettlement during and after the war, both the BCC and JUCC went through a period of disintegration and reorganization. Most churches had to start over after the war, although there was a pool of members to draw upon as churches were reestablished in new locations. Since the development of these two organizations was so disrupted by the events surrounding the war, this analysis will focus upon the nature of religous leadership and organizational change during the post-war period. It is worth recalling, however, that the BCC operated almost exclusively in the Japanese language during the pre-war period. Apart from one Canadian-born priest who served the BCC for approximately one year before the war, all priests were Japanese-speaking Issei. The JUCC was also dominated by Issei ministers during the pre-war period. Nevertheless, a bilingual minister organized the first English-speaking Nisei congregation as early as 1936.

In addition, the JUCC had the support of WMS workers who
organized English night schools, Sunday schools, and
kindergartens in a number of locations. What we must
turn to consider now is whether this tendency toward
more acculturated leadership in the JUCC has continued
in the post-war period.

Within the BCC, reliance of churches upon priests
sent from the International Department of Nishi Honganji
has persisted throughout the post-war period. As Table
V-5 reveals, 22 of 32 priests serving the BCC from 1945
to 1983 have been Issei. Thus, almost 70 percent of the
priests have been less than adequately prepared to
minister to the acculturated second and third generations. The 8 Nisei priests have on the average served
almost 4 years longer than Issei priests during this
same period. When the total number of years served are
divided among the 18 congregations within the BCC, it is
apparent that many churches have gone without a resident
priest during this period. This is due to both the
financial constraints of the smaller churches, and the
difficulty of securing priests. The two Caucasian
priests included in Table V-5, both served the Honpa
Buddhist Churches of Alberta during the period in which
they were not member churches of the BCC. Since the
Honpa Churches were not recognized as legitimate by the
BCC--the administrative authority for Jodo Shinshu in
Canada--they had difficulty securing priests from Nishi
Honganji during this time.

Although Issei religious leaders have continued to
dominate the BCC, the presence of several active Nisei
priests early in the post-war period encouraged the
process of "Anglification" in many of the churches.[8] An
examination of several indices will illustrate this
general trend toward Anglification in the BCC: the

introduction of English language services and Sunday schools, the use of English language materials (Scripture and Hymns or Gathas) for these services, and the use of English for church publications (bulletins and newsletters, for example).

Table V-5

Religious Leadership in the BCC By Generation
and Length of Service, 1945-1983

	NUMBER	PERCENT	TOTAL NO. OF YEARS	TOTAL NO. OF YEARS
Issei	22	69	185	8.40
Nisei	8	25	97	12.12
Caucasian	2	6	7	3.50
TOTAL	32	100	289	9.03

SOURCE: Interviews and Historical Records.

Table V-6 shows that all 16 of the BCC congregations responding to the organizational questionnaire have had English services for a number of years.[9] It should be noted that the nature of these English services varies considerably from church to church. Generally speaking, in the smaller churches (Hamilton Buddhist Church, for example), priests only conduct one religious service, but provide brief remarks and "Dharma Talks" in both Japanese and English. Those churches without a resident priest might only have a visiting priest once or twice per month to conduct services. In the larger churches, priests conduct separate services; one in Japanese for the Issei and another in English for the Nisei and Sansei. In the Toronto Buddhist Church, for instance, apart from one bilingual joint service each month, these separate services are held each week.

Table V-6 also reveals that English language Sunday schools have been important in the post-war BCC. All of the 16 churches have had English Sunday schools (although three have been discontinued for lack of students) and in seven cases for longer periods of time than they have had English services for adults. This observation suggests considerable initiative on the part of lay leaders in the BCC; in the absence of bilingual priests for English services, Nisei lay leaders organized English Sunday school programs for the Sansei youth.

Table V-6

English Services and Sunday Schools in the BCC
By Number of Years

CHURCH	YEAR ORGANIZED	ENGLISH SERVICES	ENGLISH SUNDAY SCHOOL
Toronto	1946	38	38
Hamilton	1946	10	18*
Montreal	1946	15	35
Manitoba	1947	13	21
Fraser Valley	1955	15	23
Kamloops	1947	30	27
Kelowna	1932	20	20
Steveston	1952	15	27
Taber	1948	15	--*
Vancouver	1951	30	30
Raymond	1929	33	41
Rosemary	1948	33	15*
Calgary	1971	10	10
Lethbridge Assoc.	1948	36	36
Coaldale	1942	20	25
Lethbridge Honpa	1946	17	17

SOURCE: Organizational Questionnaire.

NOTE: * Discontinued; --Dash means data not available.

Our findings on the other indices also show support for the trend toward Anglification. All of the churches included in Table V-6, with one exception, reported that both Japanese and English language materials were used for religious services. Again, with one exception, those churches printing bulletins and newsletters indicated that both languages were used. The exception in both cases is the Calgary Buddhist Church; it uses English for all of its religious services and for printing bulletins and newsletters.[10]

Although the Anglification process in the BCC appears to have progressed rapidly since the Second World War, Nisei lay leaders indicate that they are less than satisfied with the English-speaking ability of many of their priests. Currently, the 18 congregations within the BCC are served by 11 priests, three of whom only serve on a part-time basis. Only two are Nisei; the others are Issei who on the average have spent less than nine years in Canada. The Nisei lay leaders completing the organizational questionnaire were asked to rate their resident or visiting priest(s) on his ability to speak both Japanese and English. As may be seen in Table V-7, approximately two-thirds of those Nisei from churches served by Issei priests rated their English ability as only "passable." According to these same respondents, one of the key problems facing their churches is the inability of Issei ministers to effectively communicate with English-speaking members and their children. In spite of the language adaptations that have been made during this period, most Nisei lay leaders report that the BCC still desperately needs bilingual priests.

Table V-7
Language Ability of BCC Priests According to
Nisei Lay Leaders, 1983

	FLUENT	GOOD	PASSABLE	POOR	UNABLE
Issei:					
Japanese	15	0	0	0	0
English	1	4	10	0	0
Nisei:					
Japanese	2	0	0	0	0
English	2	0	0	0	0
N = 16					

SOURCE: Organizational Questionnaire.
NOTE: The respondent for Toronto Buddhist Church rated
both of its ministers.

An examination of religious leadership within the
JUCC during this same period reveals that a larger
number of acculturated or English-speaking ministers
have been active. Table V-8 shows that out of a total
of 31 ministers, only 16 (52 percent) have been Issei
(compared to 69 percent for the BCC). Their terms of
service account for approximately 54 percent of the
total number of years served. The seven Nisei
ministers, two of the Caucasian ministers, and the one
Korean minister have been bilingual and provided
services in both languages. The remaining five
ministers have only provided services in English for the
Nisei congregations. As in the BCC, the average term of
service for JUCC ministers has been approximately nine
years. In addition to these ministers, the JUCC has had
eight WMS workers (seven Caucasian and one Nisei)
assigned to the various Japanese congregations during
the two decades following the war. These workers
provided important leadership in the organization of

English Sunday schools, kindergartens, and, in some cases, English classes for adults.

Table V-8

Religious Leadership in the JUCC by Generation and Length of Service, 1945-1983

	NUMBER	PERCENT	TOTAL NO. OF YEARS	AVERAGE NO. OF YEARS
Issei	16	52	160	10.00
Nisei	7	23	88	12.57
Caucasian	6	19	41	6.83
Korean	1	3	2	2.00
Chinese	1	3	2	2.00
TOTALS	31	100	293	9.45

SOURCE: Interviews and Historical Records.

With a larger number of English-oriented religious leaders in the JUCC, one would expect to find that the process of Anglification has proceeded more rapidly. Surprisingly enough, the findings of this study do not support that expectation (see Table V-9). In fact, churches within the BCC have had English services offered for an average of about 22 years, whereas congregations within the JUCC have had English services for an average of 20 years. Similarly, BCC churches have provided English Sunday schools for an average of four years longer than JUCC congregations.

What accounts for this divergence from the expected pattern of development? As noted in Chapter Four, the initial policy of the United Church toward Japanese in the early post-war period was one of total assimilation or integration into existing Anglo-congregations. In other words, the administrators of the United Church intended for Anglo-conformity to eliminate the need for transitional ethnic churches. Even after approving supplementary services for Japanese Issei meeting in Anglo churches, the United Church still encouraged the Canadian-born Japanese to join the churches in their own neighborhoods. English services for Canadian-born Japanese were only begun several years after church leaders recognized the failure of the integration policy. Since there was never any intention of establishing Japanese churches that would incorporate successive generations, the organization of English services in the JUCC occurred more slowly than in the BCC.

Table V-9
English Services and Sunday Schools in the
JUCC by Number and Years

CHURCH	YEAR ORGANIZED	ENGLISH SERVICES	ENGLISH SUNDAY SCHOOLS
Hamilton	1946	26	20
Toronto	1946	32	29
Montreal	1947	33	33
Vancouver	1957	12	12
Fraser Valley	1957	0	20
Manitoba	1944	20	40
Southern Alberta	1951	9	15
Okanagan	1922	20	2
Steveston	1953	30	30

SOURCE: Organizational Questionnaire and Historical Records.
NOTE: In this table, the separate Issei and Nisei churches in both Toronto and Vancouver have been treated as one unit.

When examining the other indices of Anglification, it is apparent that the JUCC is as equally advanced as the BCC. If the separate Issei and Nisei churches in Toronto and Vancouver are treated as one unit, then all but two of the congregations use both Japanese and English in their printed materials for religious services and newletters. The two exceptions are the churches in the Fraser Valley and Steveston: the former uses only Japanese and the latter only English.[11]

Although the JUCC organized its English congregations more slowly than did the BCC, its leadership over these years has been more acculturated and English oriented. The involvement of Caucasian ministers and WMS workers certainly substantiates this observation. Those Nisei lay leaders responding to the organizational questionnaire for the JUCC tended to perceive their ministers as more competent than did their counterparts in the BCC. The 4 Issei ministers serving bilingual congregations were rated in their English-speaking ability as follows: 2 fluent, 1 good, and 1 poor.

This data on religious leadership and Anglification indicates that the wide differences in adaptation which marked the initial case studies were not representative for the JUCC and BCC across Canada. The JUCC has had more English-speaking ministers, but it has not been consistently more effective in making adaptations. Many congregations within the BCC have made adaptations more rapidly than the JUCC. Consequently, there is considerable variation within both minority church organizations in the ability to incorporate the acculturated generations.[12]

Table V-10 summarizes data on generational composition in churches located in five different provinces.

Table V-10

Generational Composition of Membership and Boards in
Selected JUCC and BCC Churches, 1982

CHURCH	BOARD COMPOSITION					MEMBERSHIP COMPOSITION				
	ISSEI	NISEI	SANSEI	OTHER	TOTAL NUMBER	ISSEI	NISEI	SANSEI	OTHER	TOTAL NUMBER
Montreal United	8	12	0	0	20	30(%)	55(%)	15(%)	0	122
Montreal Buddhist	0	5	0	0	5	8	86	6	0	80
Toronto United	30	26	6	0	62	45	33	22	0	632
Toronto Buddhist	4	25	2	0	31	35	60	5	0	800
Manitoba United	3	10	0	0	13	60	30	10	0	110
Manitoba Buddhist	1	15	2	1	19	20	70	10	0	190
S. Alberta United	4	8	0	0	12	63	32	1	3	65
Lethbridge Honpa	2	14	1	0	17	20	40	35	5	225
Steveston United	0	6	0	8	14	26*	0	0	74	116
Steveston Buddhist	3	12	0	0	15	25	70	5	0	452

SOURCE: Organizational Questionnaires and Interviews; the membership columns are
all in percentages.
NOTE: *Number includes Issei and Nisei. Statistics for Toronto United are based
upon combinations of the separately organized Issei and Nisei congregations.

The findings reveal that the situation in Hamilton was far from being representative. In Lethbridge, for example, the Honpa Buddhist Church has been more successful than the United Church in providing English services and incorporating the second and third generations as members and lay leaders on the church boards. Similarly, the Manitoba Buddhist Church also has a larger percentage of Nisei and Sansei members than the Japanese United Church. In Toronto, both churches had bilingual leaders throughout their history and have had quite active participation from both Nisei and Sansei. The higher percentage of Sansei membership in the Toronto Japanese United Church is somewhat misleading since membership criteria is different in these two congregations. Membership in the BCC congregations is based upon payment of annual dues or pledges by adult members; hence, active Sansei who have neither finished college nor have been employed fulltime would be included as official members. In the JUCC, membership is based upon confirmation and baptism rather than the financial contributions of adult members. Therefore, the statistics on Sansei participation in the JUCC would tend to be exaggerated and those in the BCC understated. In any case, the data presented in Table V-10 reveals a number of variations from the hypothesized pattern of development.

While Japanese minority churches have differed in their ability to adapt, they all have in common the need to adapt. In the following chapter, attention will be focused upon the central problems currently experienced by both the BCC and JUCC resulting from their common experience of assimilation.

REFERENCES

1.   The statistics in Table V-3 require a note of clarification. In an interview with the resident priest of Kelowna Buddhist Church I was informed that the younger Sansei tend to be more exogamous. During his three years of residence, only one Sansei out of ten has married another Japanese Canadian. The statistics for Manitoba Buddhist Church are only for those Sansei marrying within the Church. Presumably, those Sansei marrying outside the Buddhist Church intermarry at even a higher rate. The statistics for Montreal Buddhist Church are only for the years 1970-1983 and were provided by the resident priest.

2.   These case studies are drawn from my paper, "Ethnic Churches Among Japanese-Canadians: A Comparative Study," presented at the Annual Meeting of the Society for the Scientific Study of Religion, 1982, Providence, Rhode Island. It was because these initial case studies supported the patterns of adaptation suggested by the typology that it seemed worthwhile to examine adaptation in churches across Canada.

3.   The early history of this congregation is recorded in Kanada Nikkeijin Godo Kyokai Shi (1961:134-38).

4.   These activities were reported in the Minutes of the Hamilton Presbytery, United Church of Canada, 11 January 1949).

5.   This estimate is based upon several interviews with Nisei leaders; no church records are available before 1966.

6.   Although the Japanese United Church is essentially a native-oriented organization, it has had to rely on the Christian Church in Japan for some of its ministers. Still, half of the ministers who have served this congregation have been educated in Canadian theological colleges and have had a strong English orientation. The ministers from Japan have also been required to provide services in English as well as Japanese. The priests serving the Buddhist Church, on the other hand, have all been raised and educated in Japan; none were prepared to offer services in both languages.

7.   Although it appears too late to make any
difference, the Buddhist Church did begin having
bilingual services the last several years.

8.   Hofman's (1972:621) study of the "Anglification"
process in Lutheran congregations in the United States
provided helpful background for this discussion of the
language transition in Japanese churches.

9.   Data was not available for the other two churches
in the BCC (i.e., Vernon Buddhist Church and Picture
Butte Buddhist Church).

10.   The Calgary Buddhist Church is an unusual case,
and will be discussed at greater length later in this
study.

11.   It should be recalled that Steveston United Church
is the only amalgamated congregation in the JUCC.

12.   In many cases, it has been extremely difficult to
analyze the relationship between organizational adaptation and successful recruitment of the acculturated
generations. Two examples illustrate this problem. In
the JUCC, for example, ministers have been rotated
approximately every five years. If a church experiences
growth under the leadership of a bilingual Nisei
minister, it may decline during the next five-year term
under the leadership of an Issei minister who is unable
to communicate as effectively with Canadian-born
generations. Although the church reported on the
organizational questionnaire that English services were
provided during both of these periods, the quality of
the English used in services has changed significantly.
The character of the minister (whether Issei or Nisei),
and not just the offering of English services, is an
important factor which must be considered. Another
factor complicating the analysis of adaptation has been
the unexpected efforts of Nisei lay leaders in
organizing English-speaking Sunday schools for their
children in the absence of professional leadership. In
many Buddhist churches, bilingual lay leaders
established Sunday schools and incorporated a number of
Sansei even though a bilingual priest was not available
for many years.

CHAPTER SIX
ORGANIZATIONAL DILEMMAS AND THE FUTURE OF
JAPANESE MINORITY CHURCHES

Introduction

Minority churches in the course of their development encounter a number of organizational dilemmas. These are related primarily to the tension between the old world language and culture of the first generation immigrants, and that of the adopted host society. The transformation of the ethnic group through the process of assimilation generates these critical internal problems. Religious institutions are generally recognized as conservative and notoriously slow in making adaptations to changes in the social environment. The problem of adaptation is accentuated in minority churches because of the extraordinary character and degree of the generational changes with which they must cope.

In the case of Japanese Canadians, the process of cultural change has been rapid. As a result, Japanese minority churches have had to manage a very diverse membership base: first-generation members dominated by Japanese language and culture; second-generation members with varying levels of competence in Japanese, but generally most comfortable with English; and a third generation almost totally limited to the English language.[1] It is obvious that the needs, demands, and expectations of these different generations place considerable strain upon the coping skills of those in positions of leadership and responsibility.

This chapter will explore in further detail the
central problems faced by most Japanese minority
churches during their evolution in Canada. The
different ways in which minority churches have responded
to these organizational dilemmas provides the starting-
point for developing a prognosis regarding their likely
future. Although definitive predictions cannot be made,
it is possible to stipulate those major factors that are
certain to shape the future course of these ethnic
organizations.

Central Problems

The findings reported in the preceding chapter
indicated that Japanese minority churches have not been
a strong force for ethnic preservation; furthermore, it
showed that both the BCC and JUCC have had difficulty
securing qualified (bilingual) religious leaders to work
with the acculturated generations. Clearly, the
required adaptations cannot be made effectively without
appropriate religious leaders. Interviews with clergy
and lay leaders from both the BCC and JUCC, as well as
responses to the organizational questionnaire regarding
present and future problems, reveal that one of the most
pressing concerns remains that of finding religious
professionals to serve their congregations. According
to these same church leaders, another crucial problem is
the declining interest and attendance of the third
generation. While the decline in Sansei participation
is due in part to the shortage of bilingual priests, it
is important to recognize that other factors also
contribute to membership leakage. A consideration of
these key issues is a necessary prelude to the
discussion of the future of Japanese churches.

Problem of Religious Leadership in the BCC

At a time when the potential membership base of
Japanese churches is increasingly English in orientation, both the BCC and JUCC find that they are largely
dependent upon priests and ministers from Japan. In the
BCC there are currently 11 priests serving 18 congregations, only two of whom are Nisei.[2] It is clear that
the BCC has difficulty recruiting and retaining
Canadian-born religious leaders. As mentioned earlier
in this study, Issei priests serving in the BCC usually
return to Japan after relatively short terms of service.
Prior to the Second World War, Buddhist priests spent an
average of less than four years in Canada. During the
post-war period, Issei priests have tended to serve
longer terms; the average is just under nine years.
With such short terms of service in Canada, it is
apparent that many priests return to Japan before
gaining the competence in English required to communicate effectively with the acculturated generations.
What accounts for this high turnover rate within the
Buddhist Ministerial Association and the inability of
the BCC to recruit Canadian-born priests? Several
factors deserve consideration here.

One of the most obvious reasons for Japanese
priests serving only short terms in Canada is that they
find it difficult to cope with the language and cultural
differences. Most congregations within the BCC now
contain representatives from three or more generations.
The usual difficulties clergy face in dealing with
different age groups within the typical Anglo-
congregation are minor when compared to the demands
placed upon leaders in ethnic churches. Priests must
provide services in Japanese for the first-generation
members and in English for the rest of the congregation.

In addition to the demand of bilingual competence,
Japanese immigrants and their Canadian-born children
expect priests to provide different services. Older
Issei members usually assume that priests will perform
traditional rituals for which they will make the
appropriate donation. Many church members socialized in
Canada, however, have ministerial expectations based
upon their exposure to the behavior of some Protestant
clergy. Consequently, some Nisei lay leaders encourage
Buddhist priests to recruit new members for their
declining congregation by making home visits to families
who have been guests of the church on some occasion.
Most Buddhist priests in Canada are ill-prepared and
uneasy about pursuing such outgoing recruitment
activities. These conflicting expectations and language
difficulties, therefore, create tensions and pressures
which discourage long-term service in the BCC.

In the second place, Buddhist priests are usually
not prepared for their loss of status and power
resulting from their move out of the Japanese temple
system and into the lay-controlled congregations of the
BCC. In Japan, priests are related to family-owned
temples and control both religious and financial
affairs. Temples remain in the possession of the
priesthood, and are passed down from father to son each
generation. In Canada, by contrast, priests are hired
by various congregations and regarded as "employees" of
the church. This is a designation most priests strongly
resent. The relatively weak position of priests within
the BCC administrative structure is clearly indicated by
the number of votes allotted to priests and laity at the
general meeting each year. Only two of 22 votes are
controlled by Buddhist priests. For this reason, the
agenda and outcome of these meetings is largely shaped
by the attitudes and decisions of the laity. Since

priests have virtually no political power in the BCC,
one member of the Ministerial Association remarked that
"they tended to be apathetic toward these meetings." If
the status and power of priests in the BCC is compared
with that of their counterparts in Japan, it is
understandable why many priests serving in the BCC
interpret their move to Canada as one of downward
mobility.

A third factor contributing to short terms of
service is the lack of financial security. Many congregations are small and unable to provide fully adequate
compensation for their priests. Over the past few
years, a number of priests have found it necessary to
find part-time employment outside of the church to
supplement their income. Currently, three priests
serving in the BCC are employed outside of the church.
While present financial conditions are less than ideal,
some priests view their future as even more precarious.
It was only a few years ago that the BCC National Board
established a committee to consider a retirement plan
for their ministers. Without an adequate retirement
program, the BCC will continue to be plagued by the
problem of priests returning to Japan after short terms
of service. The housing arrangements of most BCC
priests compound this problem. Priests are generally
provided with a manse during their term of service; upon
retirement, they would be without a residence and lack
the income required for basic living expenses. The
prevailing discontent within the Ministerial Association
regarding these financial conditions was aptly summed-up
by an Issei priest whom I interviewed:

> If I had a comfortable temple in Japan, I
> would think of going home. When my children
> were very young, they could have adjusted to

Japanese life. But I don't have a temple and
my children are no longer young. Right now I
have no alternative and can get along in the
present situation. When we (the Ministerial
Association) get together for our meetings, a
few ministers say they are really thinking
about going back to Japan if there is a
chance.

The financial situation within the BCC has not only
contributed to short terms of service by Issei priests;
it is undoubtedly related to the departure of four
bilingual Nisei priests from full-time service. Some
years ago, two of these priests left the BCC to work in
the Buddhist Churches of America, a larger organization
in the United States with greater opportunities and more
adequate financial arrangements. As for the other two
bilingual priests, one is employed as a university
professor and the other manages a restaurant business.

One final factor contributing to the continual
change of personnel within the Ministerial Association
is related to the hereditary temple system mentioned
above. Many of the priests recruited for service in the
BCC come to Canada with the understanding that it is
only a temporary assignment. It is fully recognized
that they are obligated to return to Japan to assume
control of the family temple when the elderly priest
retires from his duties. During the past five years,
four priests have returned to Japan under these
circumstances. The BCC will continue to face this
problem as long as it remains foreign-oriented and
dependent upon priests from Japan.[3]

Over the past few years, several efforts have been
made within the BCC to solve, or at least cope with, the

recurring leadership problem. In 1979, the Toronto
Buddhist Church established a program known as
"Financial Aid for Ministerial Aspirants in Canada"
(FAMAC) in an attempt "to encourage and assist Canadian
Buddhists to pursue Buddhist studies and become
ministers in the BCC." The FAMAC brochure describes the
need for Canadian-born priests as follows:

> Since the end of World War II our churches
> have experienced a shortage not only of
> ministers generally, but of ministers able to
> communicate effectively with congregations
> which were comprised in increasing numbers of
> English-speaking members. Meanwhile, fewer
> and fewer ministers in Japan were available to
> come to Canada (1979:1).

To encourage Canadian Buddhists to train for the
priesthood, the FAMAC program will award five consecu-
tive annual grants of up to $10,000 for a student to
complete an M.A. at the Institute for Buddhist Studies
in Berkeley, California, and to study at Chuo-Bukkyo-
Gakuin (Central Buddhist Institute) in Kyoto, Japan, for
another two and one-half years. The only obligation a
recipient of these awards has is to serve a three-year
term within the BCC upon the successful completion of
his studies.

One year after FAMAC was established, the Chairman
of the BCC optimistically reported that "this program
will undoubtedly have very far-reaching effects on the
Jodo Shinshu missions in all of Canada for many years."[4]
This same chairman encouraged parents to persuade their
children to become priests. It has been five years
since this program was initiated and, as yet, there have

been no Canadian-born Japanese applying for this
generous funding to train for the priesthood. My
interviews with both Nisei lay leaders and Issei priests
indicate that most parents, rather than persuading their
children to enter the priesthood, discourage them from
pursuing a religious vocation. Because priests in the
BCC have few benefits and are poorly paid, Nisei parents
have little if any motivation to push their children
into Buddhist studies. As one Nisei lay leader
emphasized, "to become a Buddhist priest would mean a
loss of financial status for most Sansei." Another
Nisei board member compared the leadership dilemma in
the BCC to a "vicious circle," explaining that:

> We need Canadian-born English-speaking
> ministers to attract new members to our
> churches. But some of our churches have so few
> members that they can't afford to pay
> ministers enough to attract any Sansei to the
> Buddhist priesthood. What Sansei will be
> interested in sacrificing a good-paying job
> for a poor paying job as a Buddhist priest?

The lack of Sansei response and these realistic observations by Nisei "insiders" suggest that the FAMAC
program is not likely to alleviate the leadership
problem in the BCC.

Another effort within the BCC aimed at solving the
leadership problem has been led by a Buddhist priest
in Calgary, Alberta. In the early 1970s, this priest's
assignment was to establish a Buddhist church in
Calgary. With only 40 families in the congregation it
was difficult to raise the money needed to purchase a
church building. Led by the local priest, this

congregation decided to enter the restaurant business. To raise the capital necessary for this enterprise, shares were sold to churches and individuals in the BCC across Canada. While there were many against a priest getting out of the "religion" business and into "secular" activities, a Japanese restaurant was sucessfully established in Calgary. Calgary Buddhist Church holds 20 percent interest in this business to help it meet its financial obligations.

Out of this initial business venture, the Calgary priest envisioned the potential for supporting the entire BCC. He recognized that one of the major reasons for the failure of the BCC to retain priests for long terms of service was inadequate remuneration; further-more, he realized that Canadian-born priests would never be recruited as long as priests remained poorly paid and without financial security. It was decided to expand the business, with the ultimate goal of making the BCC more financially secure. Visiting churches across Canada, the priest raised the capital needed to estab-lish a larger company and gave 20 percent interest to the BCC. Over the past few years this company has been expanding and presently manages the food outlets in the Gulf Square Building in downtown Calgary, the fast-food outlets in several shopping malls, and the food and liquor outlets in the Edmonton International Airport. According to my informants, the BCC has not yet bene-fited from its interest in this company. Apparently, the profits have been reinvested for the expansion of the business. It does not appear, therefore, that this business enterprise will effectively eliminate the BCC leadership difficulties in the foreseeable future.[5]

While this business venture and the FAMAC program are two attempts to solve the BCC leadership

problems on a long-term basis, the recently organized
"Lay Speakers Training Program" is a more realistic
effort by the BCC to cope with the immediate shortage of
ministers.   Since there are only 11 priests serving 18
churches across Canada, it is clear that a number of
congregations are without a priest for many of their
religious services.   The training program was not
designed to replace the need for priests, but to prepare
lay leaders to assist in liturgical proceedings and lead
members in religious services if an ordained priest is
unavailable for any reason.

After being discussed in BCC meetings for a number
of years, this program was finally started in May 1983,
and its first three-day training seminar was held in
Calgary.   The BCC budgeted $8,000 for this program and
had five priests lead the seminars for the 17 lay
leaders who attended from the various churches.   BCC
certification as a "Lay Speaker" requires seminars and
study in the following areas:

(1) Meditation
(2) Sutra Chanting
(3) Buddhist Etiquette
(4) Ritual (Service Procedure)
(5) Fundamental Buddhist History and Doctrine
(6) Basic Pali and Sanskrit Terms
(7) Basic Japanese Terms (Shinshu)
(8) Buddhist Days of Commemoration and Memorials
(9) Jodo Shinshu History and Teaching

Even though all of these topics cannot be covered in
depth, the study program does provide lay leaders with a
foundation and knowledge of the Buddhist tradition that
far surpasses that of the average member.   This program

should benefit the participating churches, although it is not a satisfactory alternative or substitute for a trained professional priesthood. Since the BCC is a church-type organization, members expect their important religious rituals to be conducted by ordained priests with "legitimacy" bestowed by the Mother Temple.

This discussion of leadership difficulties in the BCC suggests that the situation in most churches is not likely to improve in the near future. The continual vacancies created by the return of Issei priests to Japan and the few (if any) Canadian-born priests available for recruitment will leave the BCC still dependent upon the Mother Temple in Japan. Dependence upon new priests from Japan, one Nisei explained, means "that congregations will continue to face the discouraging task of starting from scratch again."

Problem of Religious Leadership in the JUCC

Turning to the leadership problems in the JUCC, it is apparent that this native-oriented organization is in a similar predicament. As the membership base in most of these churches has become increasingly English-speaking, the JUCC has become more dependent upon Issei ministers. Like the BCC, the JUCC has had Canadian-born ministers who have left the Conference after short terms. According to my informants, two Nisei serving in the JUCC some years ago were both too assimilated to remain in ethnic churches; both had married Caucasians and were not strong in the Japanese language. Also, they were not convinced that separate Japanese churches were needed for the Canadian-born generations. In other words, they were in sympathy with the post-war integration policy of the United Church. Both are now serving Anglo-congregations within the United Church of Canada.

Currently, there are six Issei and two Nisei ministers serving in the JUCC. During the past two years, several ministerial changes have created new vacancies that must be filled: one Nisei minister, after approximately twenty years of service, moved to the United States to serve a Japanese Methodist Church; a Caucasian bilingual minister retired; and an Issei minister returned to Japan as a missionary.

As in the BCC, the problem of leadership is one of finding ministers who can provide services in Japanese for the remaining Issei members, and in English for the second and third generations. At the present time, the choice is between recruiting Issei ministers from Japan who are strong in Japanese and weak in English, or recruiting Nisei or Caucasian ministers who are strong in English but have little or no Japanese. Since the churches within the JUCC were initially organized to meet the language needs of the immigrants, it is unlikely that the Conference will abandon the Issei members during their later years and recruit only English-speaking ministers. Issei ministers will probably end up filling these vacancies and provide Japanese services for the older members and struggle with English services for the other members.

As indicated in Chapter Five, Issei ministers in the JUCC have on the average served slightly longer terms than their counterparts in the BCC. This pattern will probably continue in the future. While JUCC ministers do face similar difficulties and frustrations in serving different generations (with the exception of the JUCC churches in Toronto and Vancouver where separate Japanese-speaking and English-speaking congregations have their own ministers), there tends to be less pressure upon them to return to Japan. As a part of the United Church of Canada, JUCC ministers have more financial security since they are included in the retirement program of this established indigenous church. Japanese Christian ministers also do not have obligations to return to Japan to assume the responsibility of a family temple. One Issei minister informed me that it is difficult to locate employment opportunities back in Japan after several years in Canada. For these reasons, it seems probable that the JUCC will not have to cope with as many short Issei ministerial terms as the BCC.

Within another two or three decades, most minority churches will no longer have a Japanese-speaking membership. As far as the problem of religious leadership is concerned, the JUCC will be in a better position than the BCC. Since most congregations will only need an English-speaking minister, the JUCC can recruit either Nisei or Caucasian ministers trained in Canada. Unlike the foreign-oriented BCC, it will not be dependent upon Issei or Canadian-born priests trained in Japan. This point will be significant as the future of these organizations is considered below.

Problem of the Third Generation

Another significant problem reported by many churches within both of these organizations is the declining interest and participation on the part of the third generation. Should this observed trend be a cause for concern? Sociological studies of the relationship between age and church involvement indicate that participation varies with the life-cycle stages. The typical Protestant pattern usually involves declining participation in late adolescence and early adulthood (between

the ages of 18 and 30), and an increase in church
involvement after families are formed and there are
Sunday school age children.[6] Since many Sansei are
currently within this age category of naturally low
levels of church participation, should it not be
expected that Sansei involvement will again increase as
they complete their education, become settled in
careers, marry and have children? The unique problems
of ethnic churches complicates the situation in the case
of Japanese Canadians. The widespread pessimism of
religious leaders regarding the future involvement of
Sansei is supported by several factors.

Most churches in the BCC and JUCC will be dominated
by Issei priests and ministers for some time. Lay
leaders across Canada have repeatedly pointed out that
religious leaders from Japan are unable to effectively
communicate with Sansei and attract them to deeper
involvement in church life. Evidently, the provision of
bilingual services is not an adequate response to the
language problem. Since many Japanese churches are
quite small, separate services for Japanese-speaking
members and English-speaking members are not held.
Rather, one bilingual service is conducted which
satisfies neither the Issei members nor the acculturated
generations. Many members complain that combining the
languages into one service makes it too long and boring.
Sansei quickly lose interest in services containing
substantial portions of Japanese. Japanese churches are
in a difficult period of transition, and this problem
will not be easily resolved in the near future.
Churches need a strong English orientation to attract
the Sansei, but the language shift cannot be made until
Issei disappear from the scene and English-speaking
ministers can be recruited.

In addition to the language factor, the decline in Sansei participation in some churches is due to geographical mobility. The achievement orientation (DeVos, 1973:23) and stress upon education within the Japanese community has contributed to this problem. According to the response of Nisei leaders to the organizational questionnaire, most Sansei attend college, trade, or technical schools upon graduation from high school. Higher education has led many Sansei away from rural communities to assume professional positions in urban centres. Those Japanese churches located in Southern Alberta and Okanagan, British Columbia, appear to be suffering the greatest loss of upwardly mobile Sansei. The Japanese churches in Montreal are also losing Sansei members because of geographical mobility. Ministers from both the Buddhist and United Churches report that they are losing the younger generation because they are leaving Quebec to find jobs in areas where there is not such strong government pressure to speak French. These churches have even lost some Nisei members for the same reason. While there is some possibility that the churches in urban centres such as Vancouver, Calgary, and Toronto could benefit from this mobility, it is certain that taken together Japanese minority churches will be negatively affected by this development.

The third generation is also problematic for minority churches because of unusually high rates of intermarriage. Intermarriage rates for Sansei in both the BCC and JUCC are over 70 percent. What are the possible consequences of such a high number of exogamous marriages for minority churches? If some of these couples are integrated into the Japanese churches, the most obvious result will be a diminishing of ethnic distinctiveness or separateness. Along with the non-ethnic spouse, the children of mixed-marriages enrolled

in the Sunday school programs will not have the same
characteristics of this "visible minority." In a number
of churches across Canada there are already a few Yonsei
(fourth generation) of mixed marriages enrolled in these
programs.

It seems more probable, however, that exogamous
marriages will tend to discourage affiliation and active
participation in an ethnic church. This conjecture is
supported by a recent study of Sansei behavior and
attitudes in the United States. In <u>Japanese Americans</u>,
Montero (1980:72) discovered that exogamous Sansei
"consistently reveal evidence of movement away from
things Japanese." Some of his observations comparing
the behavior of endogamous and exogomous Sansei are
significant and worth noting here:

> Exogamous Sansei are less likely to retain
> their traditional religion, Buddhism. Only
> about one in ten of the exogamous Sansei are
> Buddhists, as against over four in ten of
> their endogamous peers.

> Over twice as many exogamous as endogamous
> Sansei report having no religious affiliation
> (26 percent and 10 percent, respectively).

> Exogamous Sansei are less likely to belong to
> any Japanese American organizations. If they
> do belong to one, it is not likely to be that
> organization to which they devote most of
> their leisure time.

> The exogamous are least likely to want their
> children to socialize solely with other
> Japanese Americans. Rather, they want their

children to take an active part in the
activities of Caucasians (1980:72-73).

In a number of different areas, then, Montero's study
indicated that movement away from the ethnic community
is "accelerated among exogamous Sansei" (1980:75). If
this pattern occurs among exogamous Sansei in Canada,
many minority churches may face a membership shortage
and be financially unable to maintain a church building
and support a resident minister.

Summary

Since minority churches are special purpose organizations established to meet the needs of a particular
ethnic group, they are dependent upon ethnic identification and loyalty for their continued existence.
Consequently, the assimilation process transforming the
ethnic group over the course of several generations
inevitably generates problems which minority churches
must solve in order to grow and survive. Generational
change is at the root of the organizational problems
confronting minority churches. "What will give one
generation a sense of unifying tradition," Yinger
(1970:112) correctly notes, "may alienate parts of
another generation who have been subjected to different
social and cultural influences."

Common problems in most minority churches stem from
the rapid cultural assimilation of Japanese in Canada.
Both the BCC and JUCC have experienced considerable
difficulty in recruiting the appropriate religious
leaders to provide services required by the acculturated
generations. "Organizational rigidity" (Starbuck,
1965:471), rather than openness to change, has been a

problem in some Japanese churches. In most cases, however, the "dominant coalitions" (Eldridge and Crombie, 1974:83) in both BCC and JUCC congregations have recognized their need to make changes; nevertheless, financial problems and the difficulty of securing bilingual ministers have frequently made organizational adaptations impossible. Failure to adapt means an end to effective recruiting and a gradual decline in membership as the aging first generation begin to disappear from the scene.

The consequences of structural assimilation are also beginning to be felt within Japanese minority churches. Clearly, the mere existence of minority churches is an indication that structural assimilation is far from complete. Still, the acculturation of Canadian-born Japanese and the reduction of barriers to full participation in non-ethnic institutions (i.e., racism and discrimination) are generating new problems for minority churches during this phase of their development. Structural assimilation has led to high rates of intermarriage among Sansei in both the BCC and JUCC. Socialization and education in the institutions of the host society has encouraged social mobility, especially for the third generation. Since upward mobility frequently requires geographical mobility, the solidarity of the ethnic community and the membership base of Japanese churches is gradually being eroded (Spiro, 1955; Montero, 1981). The pull of structural assimilation and the resulting outward movement of Sansei makes membership leakage a critical problem for minority churches as they face the future.

The Future of Japanese Minority Churches

In considering the future of Japanese churches in Canada it is important to review the social conditions under which most of these minority churches were organized shortly after the Second World War. First, the strong leadership of the Issei with their cultural and language differences provided the motivation and resources necessary for most of these churches to be established. Since Japanese language services were not offered in the existing institutions, it was only natural that they would organize their own. Second, discrimination on the part of the host society and exclusion from Caucasian churches made minority churches appear to be a desireable alternative for many of the first and second generations.

Over the past forty years, both of these social conditions have been altered considerably. Nisbet (1953:61) has suggested that "no social group will long survive the disappearance of its chief reasons for being." It seems quite clear that in the case of Japanese churches in Canada, their "chief reasons for being" are rapidly disappearing. The original immigrants will all be deceased within a few years. Many have already passed away and most have moved out of their positions of leadership in these churches. Since Nisei are generally more competent in English, and Sansei are almost without exception limited to English, soon there will no longer be a need for Japanese language services. The hostile political climate and government restrictions once faced by Japanese have also been largely eliminated. Most Sansei were born after the Second World War and were never exposed to a tightly knit ethnic community, nor subjected to racial discrimination to the degree that their parents were. For

the third generation, therefore, ethnic identity has
generally not been reinforced by outside hostility, and
dependence upon minority churches is declining
accordingly. Since the religious and social needs of
Sansei can be met equally well within the institutions
of the host society, the appeal of minority churches is
gradually diminishing.[7] In terms of assimilation, the
dynamics of minority church development can be summed-up
as follows: As cultural assimilation occurs, the
internal reasons for minority church existence are
eliminated. When exclusionary practices of the dominant
group decline and structural assimilation advances, the
external pressure encouraging minority church
persistence is also eliminated.

Organizational Dissolution vs. Succession of Goals

What is the future of Japanese minority churches
when assimilation reaches an advanced stage? From an
organizational perspective, our question is: What
happens to a minority church when its "environment
changes in such a way to make its goals irrelevant or
unobtainable" (Sills, 1968:372)? As this study has
shown, the ostensible purpose of minority churches when
they are initially organized is to meet the unique
religious and social needs of a particular ethnic group.
In the case of Japanese churches, this goal or purpose
is becoming increasingly irrelevant. The acculturated
Canadian-born generations by and large do not have the
unique language and social needs which motivated the
Issei to establish these churches. The changing
character of the potential membership base and the
decline in prejudice and discrimination has transformed
the environment in which Japanese minority churches
operate.

Over the past century, the social conditions which encourage minority church persistence have been largely removed. In light of these major changes, if minority churches continue to base their relevance upon "ethnic enclosure and support" (Kayal, 1973:424), their future is likely to be one of eventual disappearance as structural assimilation continues to take its toll. An alternative to organizational dissolution can be provided by a reorientation and "succession of goals" (Sills, 1957:257). In other words, minority churches have a "choice between going out of business or developing a new goal" (Hall, 1972:92). If minority churches de-ethnicize their religious tradition and broaden their base of relevance, organizational survival is a possibility. In order to recruit non-ethnics (and assimilated Sansei), minority churches must broaden their original goal to include these "outsiders" and create an environment which would be equally attractive to them.

It is apparent that "goal succession" is generally not occurring in either the BCC or JUCC.[8] Many Japanese churches have, nevertheless, made adaptations to meet the language needs of their own acculturated generations. These accommodations have already begun to transform the internal character and environment of Japanese churches in a manner necessary for the eventual redefinition of their goals. At least some Japanese churches, therefore, have been "de-ethnicized" gradually over the course of their evolution in Canada. It may be that in some cases, minority churches will not consciously modify their original goals or purpose. Rather, as accommodations are made to English-speaking members and Sansei mixed marriages are incorporated within these churches, congregations may slowly make the

transition from an "ethnic" to an "inter-ethnic" or
"multi-ethnic" organization.

The scenario of "organizational dissolution" or
"amalgamation" could be altered by changes in the two
social conditions mentioned above. First, the arrival
of a significant number of new Japanese immigrants
could provide a new pool of potential recruits for
ethnic religious services. Second, a new wave of racial
discrimination and exclusion from non-ethnic institutions could push some acculturated Japanese back into
ethnic churches. Current conditions give no indication
that either of these changes will occur in the foreseeable future. Since only 10,332 Japanese immigrants
arrived in Canada between 1946 and 1976 (Ueda, 1978:21),
new recruits from among the post-war immigrants will
probably have little impact on the Japanese churches
apart from the centres of the Japanese population in
Toronto and Vancouver. Several informants have
emphasized that few post-war immigrants are interested
in belonging to a Japanese organization. Those new
immigrants joining Japanese churches find that they do
not fit in comfortably with the older Issei members
whose language and attitudes were shaped by the culture
of Meiji Japan. Neither do they identify with the Nisei
members, whose character and personality were shaped by
the old Meiji culture of their parents and the childhood
experiences of rejection by Anglo society. In essence,
the new Japanese immigrants constitute a separate
generational unit.[9] The lack of interest among new
immigrants in affiliating with Japanese religious
organizations is indicated in Table VI-1.[10]

Since many of the post-war immigrants are
"technical immigrants" (gijutsu-imin), they are most
likely to settle in the urban centres where their

Table VI-1

New Immigrant Membership in the BCC and JUCC, 1983

BCC CHURCHES	NEW IMMIGRANTS	(TOTAL MEMBERSHIP)	JUCC CHURCHES	NEW IMMIGRANTS	(TOTAL MEMBERSHIP)
Steveston	6	(452)	Hamilton	5	(209)
Manitoba	10	(190)	Toronto Issei	45	(283)
Lethbridge Honpa	10	(225)	Toronto Nisei	1	(349)
Kelowna	2	(103)	Fraser Valley	16	(58)
Montreal	4	(90)	Vancouver Issei	20	(130)
Calgary	15	(150)	Vancouver Nisei	5	(45)
Toronto	75	(800)	Southern Alberta	3	(65)
Coaldale	4	(36)	Okanagan	0	(78)
Hamilton	3	(66)	Montreal	10	(122)
Fraser Valley	6	(50)	Manitoba	0	(110)
Kamloops	20	(163)	Steveston	0	(116)
Taber	14	(45)			
Rosemary	9	(22)			
Raymond	56	(100)			
(N = 14)			(N = 11)		
TOTALS	234	(2,492)		105	(1,565)

SOURCE: Organizational Questionnaire.

technical and professional skills are in demand. Most
Japanese churches located outside of these centres,
therefore, cannot count upon new Japanese immigrants to
replenish their shrinking membership base. Even the
Japanese churches in Montreal, currently experiencing
membership loss due to the geographical mobility of
Nisei and Sansei, are not likely to benefit in the
future by Japanese immigration to Canada. According to
the resident priest of Montreal Buddhist Church, there
have been no new immigrants in Quebec since 1970 because
the government requires that they speak French. It
seems probable that both the BCC and JUCC will be able
to maintain Japanese-speaking congregations in Toronto
and Vancouver indefinitely. The Japanese-speaking
component of their congregations will, however, be
shrinking as the original Issei pass away. Many of the
post-war immigrants "are university graduates and able
to converse in English" (Ueda, 1978:34). So unlike the
original Issei, they are less dependent upon Japanese-
speaking organizations (Ujimoto, 1980:137). Only a
small percentage of these new immigrants can be expected
to affiliate themselves with the existing minority
churches.

Outside of Toronto and Vancouver, therefore, the
future for most minority churches is either "fold" or
"amalgamate." The assimilation of the Sansei through
acculturation and intermarriage and the lack of
potential recruits from among the post-war immigrant
population suggest that there is no other option. Of
course, there is a natural resistance to either one of
these alternatives. After years of investment of time,
finances, and emotions, church leaders and dedicated
members will find it difficult to face the fact that it
is necessary to close a church due to membership loss
and financial problems. On the other hand, it is also

difficult for an ethnic church to change its vision and
goals and attempt to incorporate non-ethnics.

In terms of Millett's typology, it appears that the
native-oriented JUCC will on the whole be better able to
make the difficult transition from an ethnic church to
a multi-ethnic congregation. As the Japanese-speaking
Issei disappear from the scene, these churches can
recruit Caucasian ministers to serve the acculturated
generations; they will also be more naturally prepared
to incorporate other non-ethnics who are interested in
joining an indigenous Canadian church. The foreign-
oriented BCC, on the other hand, represents a religion
somewhat alien to Canada. For reasons already noted, it
will have difficulty in making organizational adaptations as well as attracting non-ethnics to the Buddhist
tradition. Obviously, the life-cycle of Buddhist
churches in areas with a larger Japanese population will
be considerably longer. The Toronto Buddhist Church,
for example, with 800 members, can shrink for many years
before disbandment would be necessary. This might give
it the extra time it needs to make the adaptations
required for long-term survival. If de-ethnicization
occurs, it may eventually be able to attract a number of
other acculturated Asian minorities with a Buddhist
background as well as the few Caucasians looking for
religious alternatives.

Thus far it has been argued that assimilation is
the dominant force shaping the future of Japanese
churches in Canada. It would be misleading, however, to
leave the impression that the inexorable forces of
assimilation will totally determine their life-cycle.
It has recently been emphasized within the sociology of
religion that religious organizations need to be
analyzed from an open-system or contingency perspective.

This approach, according to Scherer (1980:10), views
organizations as a "negotiated order" and stresses the
"importance of human actors as decision makers and
creators of policy." Throughout this study I have
recognized this important component of organizations,
stressing that the attitudes and orientations of members
and lay leaders circumscribe the degree of minority
church accommodation and adaptation. This is equally
true as these ethnic organizations respond to the more
advanced stage of assimilation. The future of the BCC
and JUCC depends partly upon the attitudes and decisions
of current members and lay leaders. Those shaping the
policy of each Japanese church must answer a critical
question: Are the religious goals, activities, and
values of this organization worth perpetuating even if
it requires the loss or abandonment of its original goal
and ethnic identity? The decisions these churches make,
along with the availability of the religious
professionals needed to serve a "de-ethnicized"
organization, will together determine the next stage of
their life-cycle. This point deserves additional
elaboration and illustration.

It is well-known that within the BCC there is a
conflict between those who want to preserve the
"Japanese" character of Buddhism and those whose primary
concern is that Buddhism survive and grow in Canada.
The Issei and many of the older Nisei hold tenaciously
to their Japanese traditions. There is a minority who
maintain that Japanese culture and traditions are not
essential to Buddhism and must be shed in order for the
churches to survive in Canada.

The only congregation in the BCC reflecting this
viewpoint in a significant way is the Calagary Buddhist
Church. This church is consciously making an effort to

eliminate some of its Japanese peculiarities and attract other ethnic groups. Its ability to do so is related to two factors. First, the Calgary Buddhist Church was established in the early 1970s to meet the needs of the upwardly mobile Nisei and Sansei moving to this urban centre. There were very few Issei among the original members, so the congregation was primarily English in orientation from its inception. Second, the first resident priest serving this congregation, though now only on a part-time basis, was raised in Canada and educated at the University of Toronto before returning to Japan for Buddhist studies. Though bilingual, he is clearly Canadian in orientation and firmly maintains that the survival of Buddhism in Canada depends upon its ability to de-ethnicize and attract those outside of the Japanese community. The Calgary Buddhist Church has taken several steps to achieve this goal. All of their services are conducted in English and the "death-oriented" Japanese memorial services, a regular part of all the other congregations within the BCC, have been discontinued (with the exception of a few Japanese memorial services conducted privately in the homes of several older Japanese in the community). Although the membership is still primarily Japanese Canadian, the more inclusive character of this congregation has encouraged others to attend. In addition to the non-Japanese spouses of Sansei, there are several members representing other ethnic groups (for example, Chinese and Thai). Issei and older Nisei are not the "dominant coalition" within the leadership structure of this church, so there is little resistance to these changes. In fact, the church board is composed of four Nisei, four Sansei, and two Caucasians. The resident priest informed me of another incident which illustrates the manner in which this congregation has attempted to shed its Japanese identity and become a multi-ethnic

congregation. When asked to participate in a picnic
sponsored by the JCCA (Japanese Canadian Citizens
Association), the church board officially declined. It
in no way discouraged Japanese from participating on
their own, but the church board did dissociate itself
from a community activity that was recognized as
exclusively Japanese. These changes in the Calgary
Buddhist Church clearly illustrate the "importance of
human actors as decision makers and creators of policy"
(Scherer, 1980:10).[11] It must be remembered, however,
that the church in Calgary is unique. Most Buddhist
churches contain members who would resist such radical
adaptations. Even if they desired to follow the course
of development being pursued by the Calgary congregation, the lack of suitable priests will make it next to
impossible for many of these churches.[12] Unwilling and
unable to make these major changes, the ultimate fate of
many congregations within the BCC is undoubtedly
organizational dissolution.

A Concluding Prognosis

The findings presented above suggest that minority
churches are prime examples of what Demerath and
Thiessen (1970:241) call "precarious" organizations:

The term "precarious" is appropriate for any
organization that confronts the prospect of
its own demise. The confrontation need be
neither intentional or acknowledged. The only
important criterion is a threatened disruption
of the organization such that the achievement
of its goals and the maintenance of its values
are so obstructed as **to bring on loss of**

identity through deathly quiescence, merger, or actual disbandment. (Emphasis mine.)

Without replenishment by post-war immigrants, the "loss of identity" (ethnic) is almost certainly the future of Japanese minority churches in Canada. In concluding this chapter, we will enter somewhat more hazardous territory and offer a more specific prognosis regarding the future of these two minority church organizations.

As far as the BCC is concerned, it seems probable that its 18 congregations will be reduced by half within a generation. Currently, there are eight churches with a membership well under 100 (Fraser Valley, Vernon, Rosemary, Taber, Coaldale, Picture Butte, Hamilton, and Montreal). Given the high rates of intermarriage and mobility among the Sansei, these small struggling congregations will be unable to survive long enough to make the transition from an ethnic to a multi-ethnic church. As it is, these small churches are financially unable to maintain a full-time resident minister. Without professional leadership these congregations will be unable to make adaptations and attract the new members needed for survival. The future of these eight churches will probably conform rather closely to the scenario suggested by a lay leader of the Hamilton Buddhist Church: "As the remaining first generation pass away and the core group of the second generation enter retirement, the church will likely fold and give its property to the BCC."

The two large churches in Vancouver and Toronto will maintain small Japanese-speaking congregations indefinitely since they can recruit at least a few of the new immigrants. But when the original Issei are all deceased within a few years, even these two largest

churches will be dominantly English-speaking. With high
intermarriage rates among Sansei in these urban centres,
long-term survival will necessarily involve de-
ethnicization. As indicted above, the Calgary Buddhist
Church has already begun to make the adaptations
necessary for survival as a multi-ethnic congregation.
The future of the other seven Buddhist churches, with
memberships between 100-450, is not readily apparent.
It depends upon the attitudes of members toward "goal
succession," the availability of English-speaking
priests, and the ability to make adaptations. What is
certain is that without new immigrants all the BCC
churches face a loss of their identity either through
de-ethnicization or eventual disbandment.

The organizational future of the 11 JUCC congregations will differ somewhat. While small Japanese-
speaking congregations will probably continue for the
new immigrants in Toronto and Vancouver, the rest of
these churches will be entirely English-speaking in only
a few years. When the Japanese-speaking Issei
disappear, these congregations can recruit ministers
from the United Church who can provide English services
and facilitate the transition from an ethnic church to a
multi-ethnic congregation. Another option exists for
the smaller JUCC congregations since they are a part of
an indigenous Canadian church. If they are unable to
maintain a large enough membership to keep their
churches operating separately, they can merge or amalgamate with other United Church congregations struggling
for survival in a nearby location. The Steveston United
Church, which formed through an amalgamation of small
Caucasian and Japanese churches in the 1950s, offers
precedent for this kind of development. Although
applauded as the first and only combined Oriental-
Occidental congregation within the denomination,[13]

Japanese leaders do not consider it an ideal model for the future. According to one Japanese minister: "The Steveston Church is a poor experiment embarked upon out of economic necessity. It is integrated, but it is not working well because the Japanese are not coming." When the two churches amalgamated, Japanese composed 47 percent of the membership. Currently, Japanese represent only 26 percent of the congregation, and on an average Sunday they represent less than 10 percent of those attending the regular service. As far as the Japanese are concerned, therefore, mergers do not represent a very desirable option as they look to the future.

Nevertheless, apart from the continuation of small Japanese-speaking congregations for post-war immigrants in Toronto and Vancouver,[14] all of the other English-speaking Nisei congregations (in Toronto and Vancouver) and bilingual congregations (in Montreal, Hamilton, Winnipeg, Lethbridge, Okanagan, and Fraser Valley) will be well on the road to becoming multi-ethnic congregations, merging with similarly declining Anglo churches or nearing the point of organizational dissolution within the next three decades.[15]

The history of Japanese minority churches indicates that adaptation stategies which insure success for the short term are in fact maladaptations when related to the original goals of the organization (Eldrige and Crombie, 1974:85). "Decisions made for the purpose of solving immediate problems," Sills (1969:177) points out, "often determine the ultimate character of an organization." In this case, ethnic churches are "de-ethnicized" as leaders decide to adapt to the needs of successive generations. When assimilation reaches a more advanced stage and the original goals of minority

churches must be displaced in order to survive, the
life-cycle of these ethnic organizations is nearly
complete.

REFERENCES

1.   Actually, the situation in some churches is even more complicated.   Some churches contain post-war immigrants whose outlook and values are significantly different from the original Issei members.   There are also a few Yonsei (fourth generation) beginning to make their appearance in the Sunday school programs.

2.   I am including in the Nisei category one Japanese-born priest who was raised in Canada and whose English language ability is equivalent to that of a Canadian-born Nisei.

3.   This discussion of factors related to the leadership problems in the BCC is based upon interviews with members of the National Board of Directors, with board members from various churches, and with priests serving in churches across Canada.

4.   Chairman's Report, National Board of Directors, Buddhist Churches of Canada, 28 March 1980, p. 6.

5.   An interview with the priest in Calgary provided most of the information for this discussion.

6.   See, for example, the summary of studies on the relationship between age and church participation by Dean R. Hoge and David A. Roozen, "Research on Factors Influencing Church Commitment," in Dean R. Hoge and David A. Roozen, eds., Understanding Church Growth and Decline, 1950-1978 (New York: Pilgrim Press, 1979): 45-46.

7.   A priest in Southern Alberta explained to me that "Issei need the church for security in the unfamiliar Canadian environment.   The Sansei are familiar with the Canadian environment and do not experience discrimination, so they have less need for an ethnic church."

8.   I will note two exceptions to this observation below: the Steveston United Church, an amalgamated congregation, and the Calgary Buddhist Church.

9.   See Ujimoto (1980:141) for a similar observation regarding the relationship between the new immigrants and the original Issei and Nisei.

10.   Ueda's (1978:64) study of post-war Japanese immigrants in metropolitan Toronto notes that membership in
any religious organization is quite low among the new
immigrants--less than 20 percent. Of those who are
members of religious organizations, 70 percent are
affiliated with Japanese-speaking churches.

11.   Information for this illustration is based upon
discussions with the priest in Calgary and the organizational questionnaire returned by the Calgary Buddhist
Church.

12.   This is not to suggest that the JUCC congregations
do not contain similar attitudes of resistance toward
abandoning their Japanese identity. Some years ago, a
bilingual minister in one of the JUCC congregations
began recruiting Caucasians from the community since
Nisei and Sansei were not attending. The Issei members
made it very clear to this minister that they had
established their church to be passed on to their
children, not to Caucasians. Although Canadian-born
Japanese were obviously showing little interest in
maintaining the Japanese church, the Issei were quite
unhappy with this strategy for survival.

13.   See the article by Rhoda Playfair Stein, "East
Meets West," in the United Church Observer (May,
1979):24-25.

14.   It is interesting to note that only about 45 of
the 283 members of the Toronto Issei United Church are
post-war immigrants. The membership of this Issei
church will decrease rapidly during the next few years.
Ninety members are already over 80 years old and another
one-third of the congregation is between 65 and 80 years
old.

15.   The Japanese church in Lethbridge almost folded
about a decade ago, but was temporarily renewed by the
assignment of an active Nisei minister who was
bilingual. Since his recent resignation and the filling
of the vacancy by another Issei minister, the future of
this church looks especially precarious. The Japanese
United Church in Winnipeg will probably dissolve with
the disappearance of its Issei members. It already uses
the facilities of Knox United Church and operates a
Sunday school in cooperation with this Anglo congregation. It seems likely, therefore, that the remaining
English-speaking Nisei and Sansei will simply become
members of the Knox United Church or join other Anglo

churches. The Japanese churches in Kelowna and Fraser
Valley appear to be in equally precarious situations.

CHAPTER SEVEN

CONCLUSIONS

Minority Church Evolution

The evidence collected in this study indicates that
the assimilation process leads minority churches through
a life-cycle of several stages. The ideal-typical
pattern of minority church evolution derived from this
study is summarized in Figure VII-1.[1]

Minority churches are initially established to meet
the needs of the immigrant generation. During this
first stage, the services and activities are naturally
dominated by the language and clergy from the old
country. The emergence of a native-born generation
leads minority churches into the second stage. In order
to effectively recruit the acculturated generation,
bilingual clergy must be secured and English services
introduced. Failure to adapt means an end to successful
membership recruitment and certain decline as the first
generation disappears from the scene. Structural
assimilation generates new problems for minority
churches and brings them to a third stage. Membership
leakage through mobility and intermarriage makes
organizational survival a critical concern. The
disappearance of the original immigrant members means
that minority churches are again in a monolingual stage,
but at this point they are dominated by the language of
the host society.

Data on the Japanese churches has indicated that
most are approaching the end of the second stage and are
beginning to face the organizational problems generated
by advanced assimilation. During this last stage,

Figure 1
Selected Organizational Aspects of
Ethnic Church Evolution

STAGES	CHARACTERISTICS OF MEMBERSHIP	ENVIRONMENTAL CHANGES	ADAPTATION REQUIRED	CONSEQUENCES FOR ORGANIZATION
First	Original immigrants Monolingual			
Second	Original immigrants and Native-born generation; Bilingual	Cultural Assimilation	Bilingual minister and introduction of English language services	Effective recruitment of acculturated generation
Third	Monolingual	Structural Assimilation; membership leakage through mobility and intermarriage; disappearance of immigrant generation	Goal succession and de-ethnicization	Transformed from ethnic to multi-ethnic organization

minority churches "must ultimately face the question of
relevance which can either be based on 'ethnic enclosure
and support' or 'a de-ethnicized religious tradition'"
(Kayal, 1973:424). With high levels of assimilation,
organizational relevance and survival require goal
succession (Sills, 1957:257) and a broadening of the
membership base to include individuals outside of the
original ethnic community. Without new immigrants to
replenish the ethnic membership base, the probable end
of the minority church life-cycle appears to be either
organizational dissolution or transformation into a
multi-ethnic church.

In applying Millett's typology to the study of
Japanese religion in Canada, I have tried to heed
Weber's (1949:94) warning against using ideal-types as
"a procrustean bed into which history is forced." Even
though the development of these two minority church
organizations did not conform entirely to the
hypothesized pattern, the typology still had an
instructive role to play. Wilson (1982:105) reminds us
that divergence from expected patterns points the
sociologist to search for other factors which will
explain those cases "that contradict our hypothesized
common-sense assumptions." In so far as Millett's sub-
typology has led to a better understanding of ethnic
organizational dynamics it has served our purpose.[2]

Religion and Ethnicity in Canada

In closing, it seems worthwhile to relate the
findings of this study in a general way to current ideas
in Canadian ethnic studies. Hansen's (1952:495) often
referred to principle of third generation return (i.e.,
"what the son wishes to forget the grandson wishes to

remember") has been expanded upon in recent years.
Isajiw (1975:136; 1978:35) argues that modern technolo-
gical society produces social alienation and identity
crises; one solution to this problem is the rediscovery
of ethnicity and a return to the social solidarity of
the ethnic group and subculture. This theory of ethnic
rediscovery supports the widely held notion of Canada as
an "ethnic mosaic" where ethnic groups and their
subculture survive indefinitely.

     While it may seem premature to reflect upon a macro
issue on the basis of this limited case study, I would
like to suggest that this image of Canada is a misnomer
as far as the Japanese community is concerned.
Progressive assimilation of each generation within
minority churches, the strongest ethnic institutions in
the post-war Japanese community, indicates that the
proverbial "melting pot" more accurately represents what
is happening to the Japanese in Canada.[3] I have seen no
evidence of a pattern of ethnic rediscovery among third-
generation Japanese. The loss of ethnic language
ability and the unusually high rates of intermarriage
demonstrate that the preservation of ethnic ties and
heritage is a low priority for the vast majority of
Sansei. These findings support the view that "Anglo-
conformity" is a dominant social reality of Canada
(Dahlie and Fernado, 1981:1).

     It is only natural to inquire whether these changes
in Japanese churches are also occurring in the religious
organizations of other ethnic minorities in Canada.
This query can only be answered definitively through
additional comparative research. Nevertheless, there is
already some evidence to suggest that the Japanese
experience of assimilation closely corresponds to that
of other groups. Even though the speed of the

assimilation process varies from group to group,[4] it appears that most ethnic churches go through a life-cycle similar to the one outlined above.

Several sociologists have observed the consequences of cultural assimilation for other ethnic churches in Canada. In a study of Dutch-Canadians in a rural community north of Toronto, Ishwaran (1977:177) discovered that English had replaced Dutch as the primary language used for religious services. The Canadian Mennonite Brethren have also been unable to withstand cultural assimilation. In the 1960's, Hamm (1978:224-25) notes, "most local churches were shifting from a predominantly German service to a bilingual or from a bilingual to English." Similarly, Palmer's (1972:239-45) study of ethnic groups in Southern Alberta showed that accommodation to acculturated generations was the pattern in all of the immigrant churches.

Structural assimilation has also had an impact upon other ethnic churches. In his analysis of ethno-religious groups in Saskatchewan, Anderson (1972:270-71) found that both Norwegian and Swedish Lutheran churches were in a general state of decline. Some churches were already closed and others had been forced to merge in order to survive. Anderson's study also reported that Ukranian Catholic parishes were declining with some churches "virtually abandoned." The type of organizational transformation projected for Japanese minority churches has already occurred in Polish Catholic parishes in western Canada. Radecki (1979:90) observed that between 1950 and 1959 "over 100 parishes and mission parishes of Polish character and with Polish clergy disappeared altogether or were transformed into multi-ethnic parishes serving the general population of

the area."[5] Although additional evidence is certainly
needed, these findings alone demonstrate that assimilation takes its toll upon the ethnic churches of other
minorities in Canada.

Perhaps these observed trends of de-ethnicization
will be reversed in the future. Some Canadian scholars
have suggested that the relatively new emphasis upon
multi-culturalism has enhanced the survival possi-
bilities of ethnic subcultures in Canada (Anderson and
Frideres, 1981:107). It could be argued, on the other
hand, that multi-culturalism symbolizes an environment
more favorable for the rapid assimilation of ethnic
minorities.[6] A review of the objectives set forth in
the government's policy on multi-culturalism over a
decade ago (1971) will clarify this issue:

1. The Government of Canada will support all
of Canada's cultures and will seek to assist,
resources permitting, the development of those
cultural groups which have demonstrated a
desire and effort to continue to grow and
contribute to Canada, as well as a clear need
for assistance.

2. The Government will assist members of all
cultural groups to **overcome cultural barriers**
to full participation in Canadian society.

3. The Government will **promote creative
encounters and interchange** among all Canadian
cultural groups in the interest of national
unity.

4. The Government will continue to **assist
immigrants to acquire at least one of Canada's**

official languages in order to become full participants in Canadian society.[7] (Emphasis mine).

The first objective shows a willingness on the part of the government to support cultural pluralism (which it has through grants for various cultural centres and festivals), but the remaining three objectives clearly foster assimilation. By assisting ethnic minorities in "overcoming cultural barriers," in learning one of Canada's "official languages," and through the promotion of "interchange among all Canadian cultural groups," the government's multi-cultural policy (if effectively implemented) would create an environment conducive to their long-term assimilation.

It is somewhat ironic to note that over sixty years ago Robert Park and Herbert Miller, in Old World Traits Transplanted, described conditions similar to those promoted by Canada's policy of multi-culturalism which would speed assimilation rather than support cultural pluralism:

If we give immigrants a favorable milieu, if we tolerate their strangeness during their period of adjustment, if we give them freedom to make their own connections between old and new experiences, if we help them find points of contact, then we hasten their assimilation (1921:308).

It could be reasoned, therefore, that other periods of Canada's history have provided the conditions most favorable for ethnic persistence. It is when minorities are without full legal rights and excluded from full participation in the larger society that they are forced to depend upon each other and develop a separate culture and social life (Reitz, 1980:204). Acceptance of minorities and their disinctive cultures, by contrast, tends to "loosen the bonds of ethnic identity" (Rose, 1964:12).[8] It seems unjustified to expect the government's policy on multi-culturalism to reverse the trends of de-ethnicization documented in this study.

Apart from the insulating and isolating mechanisms so effectively used by some sectarian groups (Wilson, 1959), ethnic religious organizations cannot be expected to preserve distinct subcultures in Canada. They are best viewed as transitional organizations that help immigrants and their children cope during a period of cultural adjustment. While there may be movements of ethnic rediscovery or revival in the years ahead, this case study has provided strong support for Coward's (1978) pessimistic outlook:

> The evidence presented indicates that they [ethnic minorities] are in danger of vanishing, of being either absorbed by the dominant Anglo-Saxon culture or wiped out by the conformity induced by the Twentieth Century technological society. It is without a doubt a time of testing for the religious ethnic minorities of Canada.[9]

REFERENCES

1.   In developing this figure I have drawn upon the
work of David Sills, "Voluntary Associations: Sociological Aspects," in David Sills, ed. Encyclopedia of the
Social Sciences Vol. 16 (New York: Macmillan Company and
the Free Press, 1968): 367-71.

2.   As Weber (1949:106) explained, ideal-types are not
intended to be exact copies of empirical reality;
rather, they are conceptual instruments useful for
generating hypotheses and comparing concrete cases.
Theoretical constructs are not an end in themselves but
the "means to the end of our understanding."

3.   I am fully aware that these popular images do not
capture the complexity of ethnicity and assimilation in
either Canada or the United States (cf. Blumstock,
1979:6-7). Since they are commonly used in the literature, I have related my findings to them. Howard Brotz
(1980:44) has emphasized the inaccuracy of these images:
"the greatest disservice that has been done to a correct
self-understanding of Canadian society has been the
invention of the fiction that the United States and
Canada differ in their ethnic relations on grounds of
'principle.' This alleged principle was that the United
States stands for the 'melting pot' which presumably
compels every ethnic group to commit suicide while
Canada stands for 'pluralism in equality'." The
salience of ethnicity in contemporary Canadian society
is not due to any profound differences in majority group
expectations in these two countries but to the fact that
"immigrants have continued to come in substantial
numbers in proportion to the total population" (Palmer,
1976:527).

4.   Sociologists have noted that the speed of the
assimilation process is related to a number of factors,
including, the degree of difference between the host and
immigrant cultures, the racial difference between the
immigrant population and the host society, the degree of
geographical concentration or dispersion of the minority
group, the comparative size of the groups involved, the
degree of institutional completeness, whether the
economy is open and expanding, the legal status of the
minority group, and the minority group experience of
discrimination and prejudice (see Yinger, 1981; Reitz,
1980; Anderson and Frideres, 1981). Breton has argued
that even ethnic groups with a high degree of

institutional completeness are eventually faced with
"leakage" as members form attachments with individuals
in the host society. While assimilation may proceed
more slowly for some ethnic groups, Breton maintains
that all will go through a life-cycle of formation,
growth, decline and disappearance (1964:205).

5.   Palmer (1972:239-245) goes so far as to suggest
that the Catholic Church itself has been an important
force for de-ethnicization, a melting pot, by bringing
together Catholic immigrants from different European
countries.

6.   In the conclusion of his essay, "The Mennonite
Experience in Canada," Frank Epp expressed considerable
skepticism regarding the government's policy on multi-
culturalism, suggesting that: "A case could be made for
multi-culturalism being another name for the melting pot
of a new, less monolithic Canadianism, a fine way to get
all minorities really to become Canadians" (in Harold
Coward and Leslie Kawamura, eds. Religion and Ethnicity,
Waterloo: Wilfrid Laurier Press, 1978:33).

7.   Originally quoted in Evelyn Kallen's article,
"Multiculturalism: Ideology, Policy and Reality,"
Journal of Canadian Studies Vol. 17, No. 1, 1982:54.

8.   Sociological insights regarding the consequences
of inter-group conflict are relevant to this discussion
of ethnic persistence and minority group cohesion.
Simmel pointed out long ago that: "Discord, in fact,
perhaps even more stringently than harmony, forces the
group to 'pull itself together.' In general, common
enmity is one of the most powerful means for motivating
a number of individuals or groups to cling together"
(Wolff, 1950:193). Elaborating upon this observation,
Coser (1956:34, 38, 90), argues that social conflict
creates and reinforces boundaries between groups in a
social system and provides the basis for in-group/out-
group distinctions. As conflict continues between
groups, their identity becomes firmly established. The
internal cohesion of the group is also enhanced through
out-group conflict since members become more conscious
of their common bonds and increase their participation
in group life.

9.   Coward's pessimism is based upon the studies
collected in Religion and Ethnicity, Harold Coward and
Leslie Kawamura, eds. (Waterloo: Wilfrid Laurier Press,
1978).

APPENDIX A

RESEARCH METHODS

Sociological research on religious organizations can be guided by three types of study designs: exploratory, descriptive, and hypothesis-testing (Scott, 1965:267). This volume began as an exploratory study with field research conducted in various Japanese churches over a one-year period (January-December, 1981). This initial period of research resulted in a comparative case-study of the Japanese United Church and Japanese Buddhist Church in Hamilton, Ontario, which focused upon the problems of assimilation and generational change. After additional fieldwork in various Japanese religious organizations in the Toronto area (including such diverse groups as Tenrikyo [one of Japan's 'new religions'], an evangelical Gospel Church, and an Anglican Church), I decided to focus my research upon the two largest ethnic religious organizations within the Japanese Canadian community: the Buddhist Churches of Canada and the Japanese United Church Conference. The study design of this larger project is both descriptive and hypothesis-testing. It attempts to describe the basic features of Japanese churches across Canada: their size, geographical distribution, membership composition, and rates of attendance at religious and social activities. It also seeks to test hypotheses derived from Millett's typology regarding their function and organizational development.

The comparative method is a common approach used in organizational studies since the controlled experiment is not possible. Blau and Scott (1962:19) point out that some degree of "control is introduced by comparing cases having strategic similarities and differences" (See also Befu, 1965; Smelser, 1973). In this comparative study, I attempt to analyze the consequences of different "administrative reference groups" for the organizational evolution of minority churches. The nature of this research problem necessarily made this study an exercise in historical sociology and organizational analysis. Historical data was used to document the religio-ethnic behavior of several generations and identify the organizational changes occurring in Japanese churches.

Several different strategies of data collection were used to obtain the information necessary to complete this study. As a "methodological pragmatist" (Burgess, 1982:163)), I applied multiple techniques to deal with the research problem, and was thereby enabled to gather fairly comprehensive data on Japanese churches across Canada.

To serve as a guide for the collection of data, I constructed an organizational questionnaire (See Appendix B). The questionnaires used by Kashima (1977) and Radecki (1979) to study other ethnic organizations were particularly helpful in designing the questionnaire for this project. In April, 1983, questionnaires were mailed to all but two of the congregations within the BCC and JUCC. The two congregations excluded from this mailing were the separately organized Issei Japanese United Churches in Vancouver and Toronto. Since these two churches serve only first-generation immigrants, generational changes could not be analyzed. I did obtain basic data on these two churches through discussions with the resident ministers which I have included in this study. The questionnaires sent out were accompanied by a cover letter and, in the case of the BCC congregations, a letter of introduction from the

Bishop. In November 1983, follow-up letters and questionnaires were sent to those churches that failed to respond to the initial mailing.

Interviews with approximately forty individuals were also an important source of information for this study. Both clergy and active lay leaders were interviewed in order to supplement and clarify the information obtained through the questionnaire. The type of interview conducted changed considerably over the course of this study. Interviews for the exploratory case-studies tended to be open-ended. During the second phase of research, however, interviews were structured around the questionnaire since specific information was required to test the hypotheses regarding organizational development. Several of the questionnaires were completed, in fact, through face-to-face interviews when I visited churches in British Columbia, Alberta, and Manitoba on a field research trip during May and June of 1983. Between 1981 and 1984, I visited other Japanese churches in Ontario and Quebec to conduct interviews and analyze various churches' records and reports. In each case I selected informants who had been active members of the church for many years, who were familiar with the historical development of their congregation, and whose formal role in the organization had exposed them to the information I needed. Most informants were serving as official board members, Sunday school superintendents, or teachers.

In order to cross-validate the data obtained through questionnaires and interviews, I engaged in documentary research. This method provided a great deal of reliable information on the history and organizational structure of these two minority churches. I should point out that the cooperation of the "gatekeepers" (Shaffir, Stebbins, and Turowetz, 1980:22) for the BCC and JUCC facilitated data collection at all stages of this study. The Bishop of the BCC was willing to write a letter of introduction to accompany my questionnaire and inform the churches of my research. A minister of the JUCC, whom I had interviewed for the exploratory case studies, introduced me to all of the Japanese clergy and lay delegates at the National Ethnic Convention of the United Church of Canada in July 1982. These manifestations of support made it easier for me when I later contacted church leaders for interviews and tried to secure various records and reports. Clergy and church officers were generally interested in this study, and, in most cases, provided access to the materials necessary for documenting organizational changes. Annual reports, church constitutions, and minutes of board meetings were among the materials supplied to me by these informants. In addition to these primary sources, two historical accounts of the BCC and JUCC were also helpful: Kanada Bukkyo Kai Enkaku Shi (1981) and Kanada Nikkeijin Godo Kyokai Shi (1969). Both texts provided data useful for this sociological inquiry on the issues of religious leadership, language adaptation, and generational composition.

Finally, archival research gave me access to materials important for placing this study of religious organizations within the larger framework of Japanese Canadian history. The Japanese Collection at the University of British Columbia and materials contained in Vancouver School of Theology Archives and in the United Church Archives, Victoria University (Toronto), were all valuable resources. The diaries, personal correspondence, government and church reports kept in the special collections afforded me insights into the Japanese experience I would have otherwise lacked.

APPENDIX B
ORGANIZATIONAL QUESTIONNAIRE

1. What is the official name and address of your church or temple?

2. When was your church organized?

3. What was (were) your reason(s) for organizing a church in your city or town?

4. How many years has your organization owned its own church building/facilities?
( ) More than 50 years
( ) 30 to 50 years
( ) 10 to 30 years
( ) Less than 10 years
( ) We do not own the facilities

5. Did your organization experience difficulty in finding and purchasing property/building due to discrimination?
( ) Yes, great difficulty due to discrimination
( ) Yes, moderate difficulty due to discrimination
( ) No, no difficulties
( ) No, we do not own a church building

6. How is membership in the church determined?
( ) Payment of membership dues
( ) Confession of faith
( ) Both
( ) Other (Please explain)

7. What is the total number of individual members in the church?

8. How many families are members of your church?

9. What percentage of your church membership is: Issei? Kika-Nisei? Nisei? Sansei? Others? (Please specify)

10. How many new immigrants (post Second World War) are members of your church?

11. Does your church and minister provide services for branch missions or fellowship groups (Please give the locations, number of individuals involved, and frequency of services.)

12. Does your church currently have a resident minister?
( ) Yes, an Issei minister
( ) Yes, a Nisei minister
( ) Yes, a Caucasian minister
( ) No, but we receive regular visits from a non-resident minister
( ) No, but we receive occasional visits from a non-resident minister

13. Is your resident or visiting minister bilingual?
Please rate your minister's ability to speak:
a. Japanese ( ) Fluent   b. English ( ) Fluent
             ( ) Good   ( ) Good
             ( ) Passable   ( ) Passable
             ( ) Poor   ( ) Poor
             ( ) Unable   ( ) Unable

14. In the history of your organization, how many years have you been without a resident minister?

15. How many years has your church had a bilingual minister?

16. Please indicate how many persons on your offical church board or Board of Directors are: Issei? Nisei? Sansei? Other? (Please specify)

17. What was the annual income of the church in 1982?

18. What was the annual expenditure of the church in 1982?

19. Please indicate what percentage of the income of your church is derived from the following sources:
Membership Dues or Contributions
Bazaars
Grants from Church Headquarters
Other (Please specify)

20. How often does your church hold religious services?
( ) Weekly
( ) Bi-monthly
( ) Monthly
( ) Other (Please specify)

21. What is the average attendance at your regular service?

22. Over the past five years has the attendance and frequency of services remained about the same, increased, or declined?

23. What special services are held in the church and what is the average attendance?

	Yes	No	Attendance
New Year's Service	___	___	_____
Ho Onko	___	___	_____
Nehan-E	___	___	_____
Hanamatsuri	___	___	_____
Gotan-E	___	___	_____
Ura Bon-E (Obon)	___	___	_____
Christmas	___	___	_____
Easter	___	___	_____
Memorial Service	___	___	_____

24. What language is used in your regular service?
( ) Japanese
( ) English
( ) Both
( ) Other (Please specify)

25. How many years have you offered services in English?

26. In what language(s) are the materials used in your religious service printed?
( ) Japanese
( ) English
( ) Both

27. Does your church print a bulletin for its regular religious services?
( ) Yes, in Japanese only
( ) Yes, in both Japanese and English
( ) Yes, in English only
( ) No, we do not print a bulletin

28. a. How often does your church publish a newsletter?
( ) Never
( ) Weekly
( ) Monthly
( ) Other (Please specify)

b. In what language(s) is the newsletter printed?
( ) Japanese
( ) English
( ) Both
( ) Other (Please specify)

29. Does your church currently have a Sunday School Program?
( ) Yes
( ) No

If yes:
a. When was it organized?
b. How many teachers are involved in the Sunday School Program?
c. How many students enrolled in the Sunday School Program are: Sansei? Yonsei? Children of new immigrants? Other? (Please specify)
d. Over the past five years has the attendance and enrollment in the Sunday School remained about the same, increased, or declined?
e. In what language(s) is your Sunday School conducted?
( ) Japanese
( ) English
( ) Both
( ) Other (Please specify)
f. What is the total number of years your church has provided an English language Sunday School?

30. If the answer to question 29 is no, has your church ever had an English language Sunday School Program?
( ) Yes
( ) No

If yes, why was the Program discontinued?

31. Does your church have a Japanese language school?
( ) Yes
( ) No

If yes:
a. How many teachers are involved in the program?
b. How many students enrolled in the program are: Sansei? Yonsei? Children of new immigrants? Other? (Please specify)
c. What is the total number of years your church has provided a Japanese language school?

32. If the answer to question 31 is no, has your church ever sponsored a Japanese language school?
( ) Yes
( ) No

If yes:
a. How many years?
b. Why was it discontinued?

33. What other programs and activities does your church organize and sponsor?

	Yes	No
Dances and socials	___	___
Trips to Japan	___	___
Japanese cooking classes	___	___
Sports activities	___	___
Annual Picnic	___	___
Annual Bazaar	___	___
English Classes for immigrants	___	___
Japanese movies	___	___
Other (Please list)	___	___

34. Approximately what percentage of your Sansei can speak Japanese?

35. Approximately what percentage of your Sansei can read and write Japanese?

36. How many children of your Nisei members have married so far?
    a. Of that number, how many married other Japanese Canadians?
    b. How many married Caucasians?
    c. How many married non-Japanese orientals?
    d. How many couples of mixed marriage attend your church?

37. Approximately what percentage of your Sansei attend college, trade, or technical schools upon graduation from high school?

This section deals with the respondent.

38. a. What is your name?
    b. What is your age? (check one)
       ( ) 26-30   ( ) 46-50
       ( ) 31-35   ( ) 51-55
       ( ) 36-40   ( ) 56-60
       ( ) 41-45   ( ) over 60
    c. Where were you born?
    d. What is (or was) your occupation?
    e. How many years have your been a member of this church?
    f. What position(s) or office(s) do you currently hold in the church?
    g. What other positions have you held?

39. What do you see as some of the problems of your church today?

40. What do you foresee as the problems of the church five or more years from now?

BIBLIOGRAPHY

The following bibliography is divided into four sections: English Books and Articles, Japanese Books, Unpublished Theses and Papers, and Archive Materials on Japanese Canadians.

English Books and Articles

Adachi, Ken. The Enemy That Never Was: A History of the Japanese-Canadians. Toronto: McClelland and Stewart, 1976.

_____. "A History of Japanese Canadians in British Columbia, 1877-1958," in Roger Daniels, ed. Two Monographs On Japanese Canadians. New York: Arno Press, 1978.

Anderson, Alan B., and James S. Frideres. Ethnicity in Canada: Theoretical Perspectives. Toronto: Butterworths, 1981.

Baar, Ellen. "Issei, Nisei and Sansei," in Glenday, Daniel, Hubert Guidon and Allan Turowetz, eds. Modernization and the Canadian State. Toronto: Macmillan of Canada, 1978.

Beardsley, Richard K., John W. Hall and Robert E. Ward. Village Japan. Chicago: University of Chicago Press, 1959.

Beckford, James. Religious Organization. Published as Vol. 21, No. 2, Current Sociology. The Hague: Mouton, 1974.

Bellah, Robert N. Tokugawa Religion: The Values of Pre-Industrial Japan. Boston: Beacon Press, 1957.

Berger, Peter. The Sacred Canopy: Elements of a Sociological Theory of Religion. Garden City, New York: Anchor Books Edition, 1969.

Blau, Peter M. and W. Richard Scott. Formal Organizations. San Francisco: Chandler Publishing Co., 1962.

Blumstock, Robert, ed. Bekevar: Working Papers on a Canadian Prarie Region. Ottawa: National Museums of Canada, 1979.

Breton, R. "Institutional Completeness of Ethnic Communities and the Personal Relations of Immigrants." The American Journal of Sociology Vol. 70, No. 2, 1964.

Brotz, Howard. "Multiculturalism in Canada: A Muddle." Canadian Public Policy Vol. 6, No. 1, 1980.

Burgess, Robert, ed. Field Research: A Source Book and Field Manual. London: George Allen and Unwin, 1982.

Clark, S.D. Church and Sect in Canada. Toronto: University of Toronto Press, 1948.

Clifford, N.K. "Religion and the Development of Canadian Society: A Historiographical Analysis." Church History Vol.38, No. 4, 1967.

_____. "His Dominion: A Vision in Crisis." in Peter Slater, ed. Religion and Culture in Canada. Waterloo: Canadian Corporation for Studies in Religion, 1977.

Cook, Francis H. "Japanese Innovations in Buddhism," in Charles S. Prebish, ed. Buddhism: A Modern Perspective. University Park and London: Penn State University Press, 1975.

Coser, Lewis. The Functions of Social Conflict. New York: The Free Press, 1956.

Coward, Harold. "Religion and Ethnicity: An Overview of the Issues Raised," in Harold Coward and Leslie Kawamura, eds. Religion and Ethnicity. Waterloo: Wilfrid Laurier Press, 1978.

Crispino, James A. The Assimilation of Ethnic Groups: The Italian Case. New York: Center for Migration Studies, 1980.

Dahlie, Jorgen and Tissa Fernado, "Reflections on Ethnicity and the Exercise of Power: An Introductory Note," in Dahlie and Fernado, eds. Ethnicity, Power and Politics in Canada. Toronto: Methuen, 1981.

Daniels, Roger. "The Japanese Experience in North America: An Essay in Comparative Racism." Canadian Ethnic Studies Vol. 9, No. 2, 1977.

DeBary, William Theodore, ed. The Buddhist Tradition in India, China and Japan. New York: Vintage Books, 1972.

Demerath, N.J. and Victor Thiesson. "On Spitting Against the Wind: Organizational Precariousness and American Irreligion," in Oscar Grunsky and George A. Miller, eds. The Sociology of Organizations: Basic Studies. New York: The Free Press, 1970.

DeVos, George A. Socialization for Achievement: Essays on the Cultural Psychology of the Japanese. Los Angeles: University of Califoria Press, 1973.

DeVries, John and Frank G. Vallee. Language Use in Canada. Ottawa: Minister of Supply and Services, 1980.

Durkheim, Emile. The Elementary Forms of the Religious Life. New York: Free Press Edition, 1965.

Earhart, H. Byron. Japanese Religion: Unity and Diversity. Encino, California: Dickenson Publishing Co., 1974.

Eldridge, J.E.T. and A.D. Crombie. A Sociology of Organizations. London: George Allen and Unwin, 1974.

Fishman, Joshua A. Language in Sociocultural Change. Stanford, California: Stanford University Press, 1972.

Goa, David J. and Harold G. Coward. "Sacred Ritual, Sacred Language: Jodo Shinshu Religious Forms in Transition." Studies in Religion Vol. 12, No. 4, 1983.

Gorden, Milton M. Assimilation in American Life: The Role of Race, Religion, and National Origin. New York: Oxford University Press, 1964.

Hall, Richard H. Organizations: Structure and Process. Englewood Cliffs, New Jersey: Prentice Hall, 1972.

Hansen, Marcus Lee. "The Problem of the Third-Generation Immigrant." Commentary (November) 1952.

Herberg, Will. Protestant, Catholic, Jew. Garden City, New York: Anchor Books Edition, 1960.

Hiller, Harry H. "The Sociology of Religion in Canadian Context," in G.N. Ramu and Stuart D. Johnson, eds. Introduction to Canadian Society. Toronto: Macmillan, 1976.

Hirabayashi, Gordon. "Japanese Heritage, Canadian Experience," in Howard Coward and Leslie Kawamura, eds. Religion and Ethnicity. Waterloo, Ontario: Wilfried Laurier Press, 1978.

Hofman, John E. "The Language Transition in Some Lutheran Denominations," in Joshua A. Fishman, ed. Readings in the Sociology of Language. The Hague: Mouton, 1972 edition.

Isajiw, Wsevolod, ed. Identities: The Impact of Ethnicity on Canadian Society. Toronto: Peter Martin Associates, 1978.

_____. "The Process of Maintenance of Ethnic Identity: the Canadian Context," in Paul Migus, ed. Sounds Canadian: Languages and Cultures in Multi-Ethnic Society. Toronto: Peter Martin Associates, 1975.

Ishwaran, K. Family, Kinship and Community: A Study of Dutch Canadians. Toronto: McGraw-Hill Ryerson, 1977.

_____. "Family, Ethnicity and Religion in Multi-cultural Canada," in K. Ishwaran, ed. Canadian Families: Ethnic Variations. Toronto: McGraw-Hill Ryerson, 1980.

Kallen, Evelyn. "Multiculturalism: Ideology, Policy and Reality." Journal of Canadian Studies Vol. 17, No. 1, 1982.

Kashima, Tetsuden. Buddhism in America: The Social Organization of an Ethnic Religious Institution. Westport, Conn.: Greenwood Press, 1977.

Kawamura, Leslie. "Buddhism in Southern Alberta," in Peter Slater, ed. Religion and Culture in Canada. Waterloo, Ontario: Canadian Corporation for Studies in Religion, 1977.

_____. "Changes in the Japanese True Pure Land Buddhism in Alberta--A Case Study: Honpa Buddhist

Church," in Harold Coward and Leslie Kawamura, eds. _Religion and Ethnicity_. Waterloo, Ontario: Wilfrid Laurier University Press, 1978.

Kayal, Philip M. "Religion and Assimilation: Catholic 'Syrians' in America." _International Migration Review_ Vol. 7, No. 4, 1973.

Koga, Sumio, ed. _A Centennial Legacy: History of the Japanese Christian Missions in North America, 1877-1977_. Chicago: Nobart, 1977.

LaViolette, Forrest E. _The Canadian Japanese and World War II: A Sociological and Psychological Account_. Toronto: University of Toronto Press, 1948.

MacDonald, Malcolm. _From Lakes to Northern Lights_. Toronto: United Church of Canada, 1951.

Mann, W.E. _Sect, Cult, and Church in Alberta_. Toronto: University of Toronto Press, 1955.

Mannheim, Karl. _Essays on the Sociology of Knowledge_. Paul Kecskemetic, ed. London: Routledge and Kegan Paul, 1952.

Maykovich, Minako K. _Japanese American Identity Dilemma_. Tokyo: Waseda University Press, 1972.

_____. "Japanese and Chinese in the United States and Canada," in Donald G. Baker, ed. _Politics of Race: Comparative Studies_. Westmead, England: Saxon House, 1975.

_____. "Acculturation Versus Familism in Three Generations of Japanese Canadians," in K. Ishwaran, ed. _Canadian Families: Ethnic Variations_. McGraw-Hill Ryerson, 1980.

Mehl, Roger. _The Sociology of Protestantism_. trans. James H. Farley. London: SCM Press, 1970.

Millett, David. "A Typology of Religious Organizations Suggested by the Canadian Census." _Sociological Analysis_ Vol. 30, Summer, 1969.

_____. "The Orthodox Church: Ukranian, Greek and Syrian," in Jean Leonard Elliot, ed. _Immigrant Groups_, Scarborough, Ontario, Prentice-Hall, 1971.

202

_____. "Religion as a Source of Perpetuation of Ethnic Identity," in Paul M. Migus, ed. Sounds Canadian: Languages and Cultures in Multi-Ethnic Society. Toronto: Peter Martin, 1975.

_____. "Religious Identity: The Non-Official Languages and Minority Churches," in Jean Leonard Elliot, ed. Two Nations, Many Cultures: Ethnic Groups in Canada. Scarborough, Ontario: Prentice-Hall, 1979.

Miyata, Kazumi. "A Capsule History of the Japanese Canadians." The New Canadian August 13, 1971.

Mol, Hans. Identity and the Sacred. New York: The Free Press, 1976.

Montero, Darrel. Japanese Americans: Changing Patterns of Ethnic Affiliation Over Three Generations. Boulder, Colorado: Westview Press, 1980.

_____. "The Japanese Americans: Changing Patterns of Assimilation Over Three Generations." American Sociological Review Vol. 46 (December), 1981.

Mullins, Mark R. "The Life-Cycle of Ethnic Churches in Sociological Perspective." Japanese Journal of Religious Studies Vol. 14, No. 4, 1987.

_____. "The Organizational Dilemmas of Ethnic Churches: A Case-Study of Japanese Buddhism in Canada." Sociological Analysis, forthcoming.

Nakayama, Timothy M. "Anglican Missions to the Japanese in Canada." Journal of the Canadian Church Historical Society Vol. 8, No. 2, 1966.

Niebuhr, H. Richard. The Social Sources of Denomina-tionalism. New York: Meridian Books Edition, 1957 (originally published, 1929).

Nisbet, Robert A. Community and Power. New York: Oxford University Press, 1953.

Osterhout, S.S. Orientals in Canada. Toronto: Ryerson Press, 1929.

Palmer, Howard. Land of the Second Chance: A History of Ethnic Groups in Southern Alberta. Lethbridge, Alberta: The Lethbridge Herald, 1972.

_____. "Mosaic versus Melting Pot? Immigration and Ethnicity in Canada and the United States." International Journal Vol. 31, No. 3, 1976.

Radecki, Henry. Ethnic Organizational Dynamics: The Polish Group in Canada. Waterloo, Ontario: Wilfrid Laurier University Press, 1979.

Reid, David. "Remembering the Dead: Change in Protestant Christian Tradition Through Contact with Japanese Cultural Tradition." Japanese Journal of Religious Studies Vol. 8, Nos. 1-2, 1981.

Reischauer, August Karl. Studies in Japanese Buddhism. New York: AMS Press, 1970.

Reitz, Jeffrey G. The Survival of Ethnic Groups. Toronto: McGraw-Hill Ryerson, 1980.

Richmond, Anthony H. Post-War Immigrants in Canada. Toronto: University of Toronto Press, 1961.

Rose, Peter I. They and We: Racial and Ethnic Relations in the United States. New York: Random House, 1964.

Scherer, Ross P. "Introduction: The Sociology of Denominational Organizations," in Ross P. Scherer, ed. American Denominational Organization. Pasadena, California: William Carey Library, 1980.

Scott, W. Richard. "Field Methods in the Study of Organizations," in James G. March, ed. Handbook of Organizations. Chicago: Rand McNally and Co., 1965.

Shaffir, William B., Robert A. Stebbins and Alan Turowetz, eds. Fieldwork Experience: Qualitative Approaches to Social Research. New York: St. Martin's Press, 1980.

Sills, David. The Volunteers: Means and Ends in a National Organization. Glencoe, Illinois: The Free Press, 1957.

_____. "The Succession of Goals," in A. Etzioni, ed. A Sociological Reader on Complex Organizations. New York: Holt, Rinehart and Winston, 1969 edition.

_____. "Voluntary Associations: Sociological Aspects," in David Sills, ed. Encyclopedia of the Social Sciences Vol. 16. New York: Macmillan Company and the Free Press, 1968.

Simpson, John. "Ethnic Groups and Church Attendance in the United States and Canada," in Andrew M. Greely and Gregory Baum, eds. Ethnicity. New York: Seabury Press, 1977.

Smelser, Neil J. "The Methodology of Comparative Analysis," in Donald P. Warwick and Samuel Osherson, eds. Comparative Research Methods. Englewood Cliffs, New Jersey: Prentice-Hall, 1973.

Spiro, Melford E. "The Acculturation of American Ethnic Groups." American Anthropologist Vol. 57, No. 6, 1955.

Starbuck, William H. "Organizational Growth and Development," in James C. March, ed. Handbook of Organizations. Chicago: Rand McNally and Co., 1965.

Steinberg, Stephen. The Ethnic Myth: Race, Ethnicity and Class in America. New York: Atheneum, 1981.

Sunahara, M. Ann. "Historical Leadership Trends Among Japanese Canadians: 1940-1950." Canadian Ethnic Studies Vol. 11, No. 1, 1979.

Sunahara, Ann Gomer. The Politics of Racism: The Uprooting of Japanese Canadians During the Second World War. Toronto: James Lorimer, 1981.

Tsunoda, Shodo, Shoko Masunago and Kumata Kenryo. Buddhism and Jodo Shinshu. San Francisco: The Buddhist Churches of America, 1955.

Ujimoto, Victor K. "Contrasts in the Prewar and Postwar Japanese Community in British Columbia: Conflict and Change," in Jay E. Goldstein and Rita M. Bienvenue, eds. Ethnicity and Ethnic Relations in Canada. Toronto: Butterworths, 1980.

Weber, Max. Methodology of the Social Sciences. trans. and ed. E.H. Shils and H.A. Finch. Chicago: The Free Press, 1949.

Wilson, Bryan. "An Analysis of Sect Development." American Sociological Review Vol. 24 (February) 1959.

_____. Religion in Sociological Perspective. New York: Oxford University Press, 1982.

Wolff, Kurt H. ed. The Sociology of George Simmel. New York: The Free Press, 1950.

Yinger, M.J. The Scientific Study of Religion. Toronto: Collier-Macmillan, 1970.

_____. "Toward a Theory of Assimilation and Dissimilation." Ethnic and Racial Studies Vol.4, No. 3, 1981.

Yoshida, Y. "Causes of Japanese Emigration." Annals of the American Academy of Social and Political Science Vol. 34 (September), 1901.

Young, C.H. and H.R. Reid. The Japanese Canadians. Toronto: University of Toronto Press, 1938.

Zald, Mayer N. and Patricia Denton. "From Evangelism to General Service: The Transformation of the YMCA." Administrative Science Quarterly Vol. 8, 1963.

Japanese Books

Ikuta, Shinjo. Kanada Bukkyokai Enkaku Shi (A History of the Buddhist Churches of Canada). Toronto: Buddhist Churches of Canada, 1981.

Kanada Nikkei Jin Godo Kyokai Shi, 1892-1959 (A History of the Japanese Congregations of the United Church of Canada). Toronto: Japanese United Church Conference, 1961.

Raymond Bukkyokai Shi (History of Raymond Buddhist Church). Raymond, Alberta: Raymond Buddhist Church, 1970.

Shimpo, Mitsuru. Nihon No Imin: Nikkei Kanada Jin Ni Mirareta Haiseki To Tekio (Japan's Emigrants: Exclusion and Adaptation As Seen in Japanese Canadians). Tokyo: Hyoron-Sha, 1977.

Tsunemitsu, Kozen. Nihon Bukkyo Tobei Shi (A History of Japanese Buddhism in America). Tokyo: Bukkyo Shuppan Kyodo, 1964.

Unpublished Theses and Papers

Anderson, Alan B. "Assimilation in the Bloc Settlements of North-Central Saskatchewan: A Comparative Study of Identity Changes Among Seven Ethno-Religious

Groups in a Canadian Prairie Region." Ph.D. dissertation, University of Saskatchewan, 1972.

Hamm, Peter Martin. "Continuity and Change Among
Canadian Mennonite Brethren, 1925-1975: A Study of
Socialization and Secularization in Sectarianism."
Ph.D. dissertation, McMaster University, 1978.

Horinouchi, Isao. "Americanized Buddhism: A Sociolo-
gical Analysis of a Protestantized Japanese
Religion." Ph.D. dissertation, University of
California, Davis, 1973.

Izumi, Yasuo. "Buddhists in British Columbia."
Vancouver Buddhist Church, 1983.

Makabe, Tomoko. "Ethnic Group Identity: Canadian Born
Japanese in Metropolitan Toronto." Ph.D. dissertation, University of Toronto, 1976.

Mitsui, Tadashi. "The Ministry of the United Church
Amongst Japanese Canadians in B.C., 1892-1949."
S.T.M. thesis, Union College, Vancouver, 1964.

Nakayama, T.M. "Anglican Japanese Missions in Canada:
A Historical Survey." M.A. thesis, Anglican
Theological College of British Columbia, 1956.

Shimpo, Mitsuru. "The Deceased and the Living:
Changing Aspects of Ancestor Worship in Japan."
Paper at the Annual Meeting of the Association for
the Sociology of Religion, Toronto, Ontario, 1981.

Sumida, Regenda. "The Japanese in British Columbia."
M.A. thesis, University of British Columbia, 1935.

Ueda, Yoko. "Post-War Japanese Immigrants in Metro-
politan Toronto: Process of Acculturation and
Social Integration." M.A. thesis, University of
Toronto, 1978.

Archive Materials on Japanese Canadians

University of British Columbia, Special Collections,
Japanese Canadian Collection:
"Hayashi Collection."
"Miyazaki Collection."

"NJCCA Collection."
"Rev. Kosaburo Shimizu Collection."
"Yasutaro Yamaga Collection."

Vancouver School of Theology, United Church Archives:
"Digest of the Minutes of the Conference of Japanese
Workers, September 30, 1943."
"A History of Steveston United Church." Rev. F.E.
Runnals, 1965.

Victoria University, Toronto, Ontario, United Church
Archives:
McWilliams, Rev. W.R. "Report of the Itinerary of
Rev. W.R. McWilliams" (in Relocation Centers),
October 19, 1943.
Shimizu, Rev. K. "Report on the Resettlement of
Japanese Canadians," June 21, 1944.

INDEX

CANADIAN STUDIES